Sycamore

Bird's Eye Maple

East Indian Satinwood

Cherry

English Burr Walnut

English Plain Walnut

French Plain Walnut

American Black Walnut

A GUIDE TO
ENGLISH ANTIQUE FURNITURE
CONSTRUCTION & DECORATION 1500-1910

A GUIDE TO
ENGLISH ANTIQUE FURNITURE

CONSTRUCTION & DECORATION 1500-1910
STAN LEAROYD

VNR VAN NOSTRAND REINHOLD COMPANY
NEW YORK   CINCINNATI   TORONTO   LONDON   MELBOURNE

Copyright © 1981 Stan Learoyd
Library of Congress Catalog Card Number 81-3074
ISBN 0-442-25952-2

Printed in Great Britain

Published by Van Nostrand Reinhold Company
A division of Litton Educational Publishing, Inc.
135 West 50th Street, New York, NY 10020, U.S.A.

749.22
L62g

16 15 14 13 12 11 10 9 8 7 6 5 4 3 2 1

Library of Congress Cataloging in Publication Data

Learoyd, Stan.
    A guide to English antique furniture construction
and decoration, 1500-1910.
    Includes index.
    1. Furniture — England.   I. Title.
NK2528.L4   749.22   81-3074
ISBN 0-442-25952-2   AACR2

Contents

Introduction

The purpose of this book is to pass on fifty years of personal and practical experience. It is hoped that the dealer and collector will find it useful for reference, but it is written mainly with the young furniture restorer in mind who, apart from being a competent furniture maker, must also have practical experience in carving, colouring, polishing and finishing, lacquering, gilding and metalwork, which will involve a great amount of study and practice. A thorough knowledge of period furniture construction and decoration is needed to be a really competent restorer, and it is hoped that this book will help attain this. Such knowledge can only otherwise be obtained through years of practical experience.

There is very little English furniture which has survived from the fifteenth century and what has is mainly of ecclesiastical origin. It consists of a small number of crudely constructed cupboards, chests, and benches or stools. Any other domestic furniture in use at this period was so crude that it could hardly be classed as furniture, although it is known that a small amount of furniture was brought in from the Continent. This book therefore, is only concerned with English furniture made after A.D. 1500.

The 16th century

Early Tudor 1500–1550, Late Tudor or Elizabethan 1550–1603

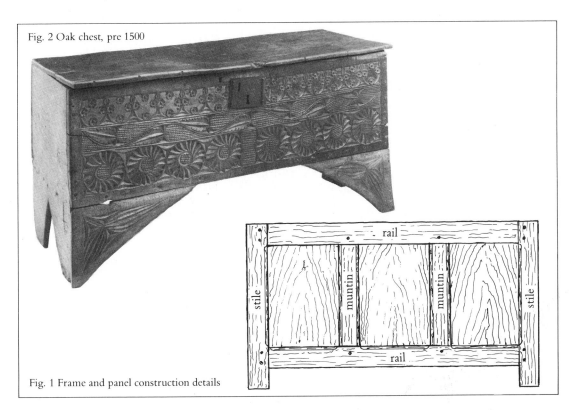

Fig. 2 Oak chest, pre 1500

Fig. 1 Frame and panel construction details

rail

stile

muntin

muntin

stile

rail

Chests

Although glue is found occasionally, it appears to have been little used until the seventeenth century. Therefore, furniture made in the sixteenth century was mainly of frame and panel construction, the mortice and tenon joints held together by boring and driving wood pins through them, known as dowelling. The wood pins were cut off flush to the surface, Fig. 1 and the fact that they now protrude is because of the shrinkage of the construction timbers.

In some of the early chests the ends and backs were solid boards which were fixed to the legs or stiles by dowelling, boring and driving in wood pins, others were fixed only by iron nails, Fig. 2. The bottoms were made up of boards dry-butted together with the grain usually running from back to front. They were fixed either by nailing in a rebate, fitting into a plough, or nailing straight on to the bottom of the frames.

9

Cupboards

These were crudely made using a panel and frame construction, the stiles extending to form the legs, Fig. 3. The heights of the cupboards varied from 90–150cm (3–5ft) and the width from 90–120cm (3–4ft). The fronts were carved and some of the panels were pierce fretted, Fig. 4. Alternatively, panels were omitted and the area spaced out with turned spindles instead, Fig. 5. The doors were hinged with metal strap hinges on the front

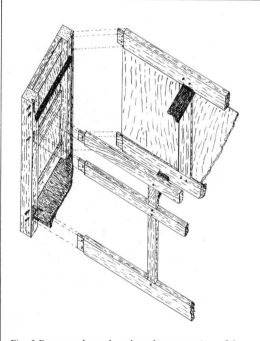

Fig. 3 Frame and panel cupboard construction of the sixteenth and seventeenth century

Fig. 4 Food or dole cupboard, c.1500

face, fixed with hand-wrought iron nails, either driven through and clinched on the rear side, or with a pivot wood or metal pin at the top and bottom edges. The latch, if any, was a wood turn-button, while some had wood opening knobs. These cupboards were used for storing food and are often called dole cupboards.

Chairs

The joint construction of chairs was the same as chests, namely dry mortice and tenons fixed with wood pins, Fig. 6, but although panel construction was used for the backs, usually with the stiles extended to make the back legs, this method was not always used for the sides and front. The front legs were often turned on a lathe leaving square sections at the bottom, at the seat rail level and, if the leg extended up to the arm, a square at the top also, Fig. 7.

The seats were of solid timber, fastened to the

Fig. 5 Food or dole cupboard, c.1600

Fig. 6 Oak chair of frame and panel construction, 1574

11

top edges of the rails with wood pins or nails, and the edges which showed were either rounded or moulded. These rails were sometimes fretted on the bottom edge. Stretcher rails were fitted at the bottom of the legs making a frame the same as the seat rails. The arms were usually a rough extended scroll shape, sometimes upright, sometimes laid flat.

Stools and benches

The early stools and benches had solid end uprights as legs and these were usually fretted and shaped rather crudely. A rail, edgeway up and central on the underside of the top, was morticed through the two legs. The tenon extended so that a hole could be bored through it close to the outside face of the leg for a wood pin or wedge to be driven in to hold the leg tight up to the shoulders of the tenon. The top, which was moulded or chamfered on the outside top edges, was fixed with wood pins or nails on to the top edges of the legs and to the central rail.

An alternative method of fixing the rail to the legs was for the rail to be trenched on both sides 7–10cm (3–4in) from each end, and the legs cut and slotted in to the trenches. Occasionally stools or benches were made with two rails fitted instead of the one central rail, Fig. 8. In the last quarter of the sixteenth century a small number of stools were made with four turned legs and rails, morticed and tenoned in square frame construction, with stretcher rails in the same form. The tops of the stools were moulded and fixed with wood pegs.

Fig. 7 Carved oak panel-back chair, c.1660

Fig. 8 Oak stool, pre 1600

Fig. 9 Detail of dining table pedestal, pre 1500

Tables

The only tables which appear to have been made in the first half of the sixteenth century, had loose tops laid on two or more pillar-type pedestals. They are known as trestle tables, Fig. 9. A number of these tables were also made with construction identical to the benches or stools, with solid fret-edged legs connected together with a slot-in central rail and a loose top. All trestle tables were heavy and solid in construction with tops approximately 7cm (3in) in thickness.

In the second half of the sixteenth century, table construction developed in the same way as stools, with four or more turned legs connected together by rails at the top and stretchers at the foot; the top was fixed on to this rectangular frame with wood pins, Fig. 10.

Fig. 10 Oak dining table with column legs and plain stretchers, c.1650

13

Fig. 11 Oak bed with tester and carved panelled headboard, c.1525

Beds

Sixteenth century beds were of the four-poster type with a canopy or tester and curtains which could be drawn to enclose the occupants completely, Fig. 11. These curtains were fixed on sliding rings and were usually made from linen, silk, satin or velvet, and were well-lined to keep out the draughts.

The posts, made from oak or walnut, were usually decorated with carving on their entire length. The mattresses, filled with either straw or wool, were held in position by boring holes in the wooden bed rails and threading rope through from side to side and end to end. Finally, one or more feather mattresses were laid on to give extra comfort.

The early bed posts appear to have been approximately 13cm (5in) in round or octagon section, later posts having a large bulbous section in the centre of the upper half, in cup and cover shape approximately 25cm (10in) in diameter, Appendix 1, Fig. G.

The headboards and tester were of frame and panel construction, and the headboard often extended to the height of the tester and supported it. Both the headboard and canopy were ornamented with carving.

Timber

The construction material mainly used was oak, but elm, chestnut and walnut were used occasionally. Woods used for inlaying, etc., were ash, beech, bog oak, fruit woods, holly, poplar, sycamore and yew.

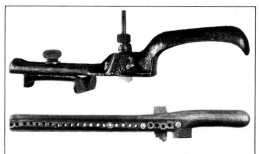

Fig. 12 Scratch-stock tools used for shaping moulds

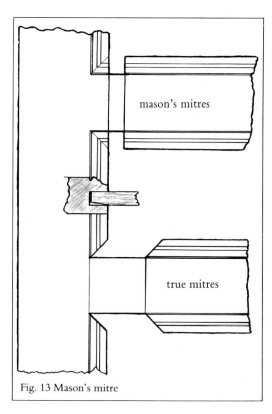

mason's mitres

true mitres

Fig. 13 Mason's mitre

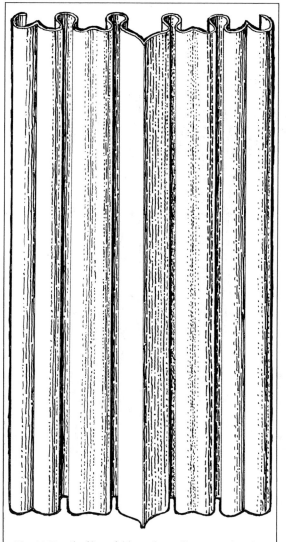

Fig. 14 Detail of linenfold panel, usually prepared with a scratch-stock

Decoration

Three techniques were used for decoration:

Moulding This was worked with a tool called a scratch-stock, Fig. 12, a wooden holder slotted with a saw to receive the metal moulding cutter, and a wooden guide piece fixed on the underside which was held up to the side of the leg, rail, stile or panel on which the mould was to be worked. There was a certain amount of unevenness in the finish using this method but this seems to attract rather than detract from its appearance.

The mouldings on the stiles or legs were usually tapered out to nothing where they were met by the rail but occasionally a 'mason's mitre' was used, Fig. 13. The mitre angle was worked on the stile, with the return meeting the mould on the rail. The scratch-stock was also used to mould the face of the panels, with the ends of the mould cut back to resemble folded material, a decoration known as linenfold, Fig. 14.

Carving This can be divided into three separate types. Chip-carving where the designs are cut into the flat surface of the wood, usually in geometrical shapes. For example, the rosettes carved on the panels in Fig. 4, page 10. Relief carving where the timber surrounding the carving was cut back to form the background, the carving standing from 5–20mm (¼–¾in) proud. These were usually figures, figure-heads or floral designs as shown in the stiles in Fig. 5, page 11. Finally, carving in the round, usually animals or human figures, the figure standing forward and showing the third dimension or thickness.

Inlaying   This is a method of fitting back into the solid timber various coloured woods to form geometrical or floral designs and it came into general use at the end of the sixteenth century, Fig. 15, although samples of chests decorated in this manner do date back to the first half of the century, probably made by Flemish craftsmen, Fig. 16. Inlaying should not be confused with marquetry, where thin veneers of various woods are made up into a complete panel which is then glued on to the solid surface. Marquetry was not used in England until after the Restoration, the second half of the seventeenth century.

Polishing and finishing   The surface finishing during the sixteenth century was confined to waxes and oils, probably to exclude the damp and to act as a preservative rather than to improve the appearance of the furniture. Linseed, poppy or nut oil were used. Beeswax was applied by rubbing the block of wax on the timber surface and then levelling and burnishing with a coarse cloth or brush. An alternative method was to dissolve the wax with turpentine to a thin paste and spread it over the surfaces with a cloth or brush. After the wax had hardened, it was burnished.

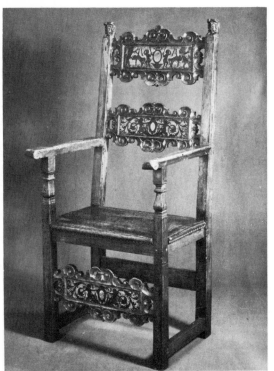

Fig. 15 Oak chair showing the use of inlaying, c.1650

Fig. 16 'Nonesuch chest', an example of inlaying with various woods and probably the work of German craftsmen

The 17th century

Early Stuart or Jacobean 1603–1649, and Commonwealth 1649–1660

During the first half of the seventeenth century, furniture-making was carried out by joiners as it had been in the sixteenth century. During the century, however, great advances were made in furniture construction and design and it is obvious that more thought was given to individual needs in the home. Around 1660 was the beginning of the craft of 'cabinet making' and, as this coincides with the commencement of what is commonly called the walnut period, it will be dealt with in the next chapter.

Chests, cupboards and dressers
From about the beginning of the seventeenth century people started to accumulate possessions and began to realise the necessity of having extra storage furniture in their homes. Therefore, food cupboards, court cupboards, buffets, dressers and presses were made by the joiners.

The food cupboards, though similar in design to those of the sixteenth century, had a more professional finish, usually with a frieze and cornice, Fig. 17, although some were made with a shelf area in front of the top cupboard, with pillars supporting the front end of the frieze and cornice in the same manner as the court cupboards.

Fig. 17 Food or dole cupboard, c.1680

Buffets and court cupboards were of two or three-tier design. The buffets were usually just two or three shelves with underframes supported at the front corners by carved or turned columns, while the back corners were usually supported by flat pilasters or panelling, Fig. 18.

The two-tier court cupboards usually had columns supporting the front of the cornice while the rear part of the top section was a

Fig. 18 Buffet or sideboard with gryphon and turned columns, c.1610

cupboard, often with canted corners or ends, leaving a shelf area at the front. The lower section was either completely enclosed by a cupboard, or just a shelf with columns or pilasters supporting the upper section, Fig. 19. The three-tier court cupboards were similar to the two-tier cupboards in the two lower sections, but with an open shelf top section with columns supporting the cornice at the front and a complete panelled back supporting the rear of the cornice.

Fig. 19 Court cupboard with cup and cover columns, c.1620

19

Fig. 20 Oak wardrobe with chest construction in lower section, c.1650

The presses or wardrobes of the Jacobean period had a box-type carcase of frame and panel construction with a cornice and frieze, and the feet were usually an extension of the carcase stiles. The interiors were fitted with shelves and these were enclosed with doors in the upper section. A fixed panelled frame enclosed the lower section making a chest-like compartment, Fig. 20. Alternatively, two doors replaced the fixed panelled frame.

The dressers of this period varied considerably in style, but they can be divided into two groups.

The first group have a framed carcase enclosing a single row of drawers along the full length of the underside of the top. The carcase is supported by four or more column legs with square frame stretchers at the lower end which sometimes supported a shelf, Fig. 21. The second group have a framed carcase reaching from the underside of the top almost to the floor and supported by short feet, which were usually an extension of the carcase stiles, or sometimes with a board plinth. The whole of the front of the carcase was enclosed by doors, often with fielded panels, and drawers. These were fitted in a variety of layouts; sometimes with a row of drawers at the top and cupboards underneath, or with drawers down the centre and cupboards at each side, Fig. 22, or this was reversed and a cupboard was put in the centre, flanked by drawers.

Fig. 21 Welsh-style dresser with legs and stretchers, c.1700

Fig. 22 Yorkshire or Lancashire dresser with plinth feet, c.1710

21

Chairs

Frame and panel construction for chairs continued right through the first half of the seventeenth century but alongside it, from approximately the beginning of the century, came the upholstered chair with a padded pin-cushion back panel and a padded seat, Fig. 23, and the upholstered settee, Fig. 24. The covers were of leather, velvet, or hand embroidered and were taken right over to completely cover the rails of the seat. They were edged with either a braid trimming or close-nailed with brass dome-head nails.

In country districts chair design began to take on a distinctive style for particular areas – notably Derbyshire, Fig. 25, Yorkshire, Fig. 26 and Lancashire, Fig. 27.

Fig. 23 Column-leg chair and stool with upholstered cushion seat and fringes, c.1620

Fig. 24 Settee *en suite* with Fig. 23

Fig. 25 Derbyshire-style oak chair, c.1650

Fig. 26 Yorkshire-style oak single chair and arm chair, c.1650

Stools, benches and settles

The construction of benches and stools continued in much the same manner as those of the late sixteenth century, but with bobbin turnings, Fig. 28 and spiral twists, Fig. 29 replacing the column-turned legs.

Settles took three different forms, the first with the lower part like a chest, in frame and panel construction with a fixed or hinged seat and a frame panelled back. The front legs of the chest section were extended to form the uprights for the arms, which were of scroll form, Fig. 30. The second was similar to the first but with a solid back which folded down on to the arms to form a table. The third came in the form of a long stool with turned legs, the front legs extended to form the arm uprights; the back was framed and panelled and the seat was solid wood. In some of the later ones the seat and back were upholstered in leather, often with leather arm pads.

Fig. 27 Lancashire-style pair of oak chairs, c.1650

Fig. 30 Oak settle with box seat, c.1650

Fig. 28 Oak stool with bobbin turnings, c.1660

Fig. 29 Walnut stool with
spiral-twist turnings, c.1680

Tables

The rectangular dining tables appear to have varied very little in style from those of the sixteenth century, having cup and cover or column-shaped legs, Appendix 1, Fig. G and I and square frames with low stretcher rails. One addition was made, however, the draw-leaf top; making possible, if desired, an increase in the length of the top of the table of approximately two thirds, Fig. 31.

Fig. 31 Oak draw-leaf dining table, c.1600

Side tables during the first half of the seventeenth century were constructed and styled on the same lines as the rectangular dining tables. Gate-leg tables for dining appear to have become very popular in the second half of this century. They varied in length when open from 150–240cm (5–8ft) and were oval or round in shape, with column, bobbin or spiral-twist legs. The earliest stretchers were square in section with the top edges rounded or moulded, Fig. 32, but later they were made to match the legs, Fig. 33. One or two gate-legs were fitted at each side to swing out and support the hinged leaf.

A small number of side tables and occasional tables with gates were in use in the first half of the century. The side tables were of the flap-top type, with the gate-leg swinging with metal hinges or wood pin pivots from the back rail and stretcher, Fig. 34. The occasional tables were usually smaller copies of the gate-leg dining tables, with four, fixed, bobbin or column legs and two matching gate-legs, but some were made with panel board ends on a foot, which made the complete end leg an inverted T-section, similar in appearance to the legs on the early sixteenth century trestle tables, Fig. 35. A wide flat board stretcher connected the two ends together and it was from this and the top rail that the two gates pivoted.

Fig. 32 Small gate-leg table with column turnings and square stretchers, c. 1650

Fig. 33 Small gate-leg table with column turnings and turned stretchers, c.1670

Beds

The construction of beds in the first half of the seventeenth century was very much in the style of those of the sixteenth. The drapings were probably more ornate and the underside of the canopy or tester, instead of showing wood panelling, was lined with elaborate needlework material and trimmings; a low headboard covered with matching needlework replaced the high, panelled headboard. Plain posts covered with material held up the head end of the tester instead, Fig. 36. Curtaining enclosed the head of the bed as well as the sides and the foot.

Timber

Oak was used extensively in the construction of cabinets, beds and tables, and in a more limited way for chairs, usually confined to the frame constructed chairs. Beech was mainly used for chair making and was usually finished with black colour as described on page 30.

Fig. 34 Flap-top, gate-leg table, c.1630

Fig. 35 Small gate-leg table with panel end supports, c.1650

Fig. 36 Bed with upholstery-covered tester, low headboard and draw curtains, c.1690

27

Walnut was in use in a limited way over the first half of the seventeenth century, and was confined to the better quality furniture. Elm was used in chest and chair making but not in any great quantity.

Decoration
Carving was used in abundance throughout the whole of the Jacobean period, and a particular feature of this was the use of the S-scroll which is a reminder of the Stuart period, Fig. 37. Inlaying was still a method of decoration, but only for high quality furniture.

Applied moulds and split turnings were types of decoration and, though used a little in the latter part of the sixteenth century, became really popular in the Jacobean period. The method was to mould straight lengths of timber, and then cut and arrange them in decorative designs on doors, drawers or panels, by gluing or nailing. The split turnings were used as extra decoration on pilasters, stiles, etc., Fig. 38.

Drawer construction in the late sixteenth century was in crude box form, the edges of the drawer fronts being rebated to receive thick sides of approximately 20mm (¾in) thick. The bottom edge of the drawer fronts was rebated to receive the bottom, approximately 12mm (½in) thick. The sides were nailed to the front, the back was nailed

Fig. 37 An example of S-scroll carving

Fig. 38 Cupboard with decorative moulds and split turnings, c.1660

on to the sides, the bottom was nailed under the front, back and sides and the sides were ploughed centrally from back to front to take the drawer runner which was fixed on the carcase, Fig. 39. In the early seventeenth century, crude, single dovetail joints sometimes replaced the nailed side joints, Fig. 40.

From about 1650 drawer sides became thinner and were fixed to the fronts and backs with a group of dovetails, the bottoms being ploughed into the sides and front, Fig. 41. The runners were so fitted on the carcase that the drawers could run on top of them.

Fittings Hinges were usually iron and became more ornate and formed part of the decoration on cabinets in the early part of the seventeenth century, Fig. 42. They were face fixed with hand-wrought nails. Towards the middle of the century brass hinges, fixed with brass pins, started to be used.

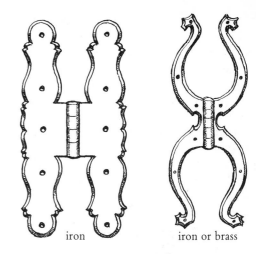

iron   iron or brass

Fig. 42 Hinges from the sixteenth and seventeenth century

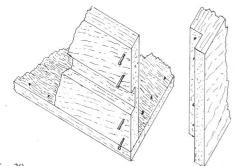

Fig. 39

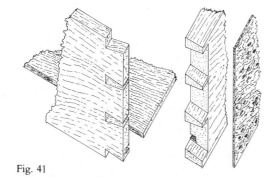

Fig. 41

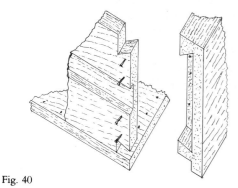

Fig. 40

Fig. 39 Drawer construction of the sixteenth to mid-seventeenth century. Diagram shows the front rebated for sides and bottom and the side rebated to receive drawer runner.

Fig. 40 Drawer construction with single dovetail joint, c.1600–1660

Fig. 41 Drawer construction, c.1660–1700. Front and sides ploughed to receive bottom and the front veneered cloaking the dovetails

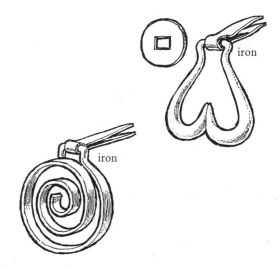

iron

iron

Fig. 43 Handles

Handles were first made of wrought iron in strip-scroll or ring form, fixed with a split pin which was looped round the pivot bar of the handle and then through a hole bored in the door or drawer. The two ends of the pin were then opened and hammered flat on the inside face of the door or drawer, Fig. 43. Metal knobs were used on drawers and doors, but wood knobs were more usually fitted.

Polishing and finishing Staining was in very limited use in the Jacobean period and was confined to concoctions made with pigment powders such as lamp black. Most of the beech chairs were finished black and this was achieved by mixing lamp black with glue size and painting it over the surface. The black surface, when dry, was polished with a mixture of beeswax and lamp black. Other furniture which was not black finished was treated with oils or wax as in the Tudor period, see page 16.

Alkanet-root dye, which came from the Egyptian henna shrub, was bright red in colour and was mixed with oil and applied to walnut. Tripoly powder, decomposed limestone, was mixed with oil for finishing walnut, but to get the lustre required was a long and arduous process and it could only have been used on the more expensive furniture.

Walnut cabinet, once the property of Archbishop Laud (1573–1645)

The Walnut period

Charles II 1660–1685;   James II 1685–1688;
William & Mary 1689–1702;   Queen Anne 1702–1714;
George I 1714–1727

The advent of the craft of cabinet making at the beginning of this period revolutionised the design and construction of furniture and its importance cannot be underestimated.

Cupboards, chests, dressers, presses and wardrobes

Cupboard design changed little in general appearance in the early walnut period, but later they were constructed with solid timber, oak or pine and veneered with walnut instead of being of frame and panel construction. The doors, though still framed, usually had their panels fixed flush to the front of the frame by ploughing both the frame and the panel and using a loose tongue or lath to connect the two together, thus enabling the whole of the front of the door to be veneered as one complete surface. The panel was usually the same thickness as the frame so that the inside of the door was the same as the outside, Fig. 44. An addition was made to the cornice of a fretted and moulded pediment usually with turned finials at the ends and centre, Fig. 45. Instead

of extended stiles forming the legs, a base mould was fitted on the underside of the carcase and the feet were turned bun-shape, Appendix 1, page 120.

Towards the end of the seventeenth century cupboards were made from two carcases with a mould dividing the top carcase from the bottom one. The top of the upper carcase was often domed or double domed with the cornice mould following the shape, Fig. 46.

Fig. 44 Two-tier cabinet of solid construction, veneered in walnut and standing on bun feet, c.1690

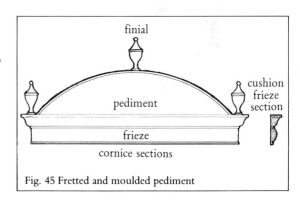

Fig. 45 Fretted and moulded pediment

Fig. 46 Walnut bureau bookcase with double-dome cornice and finials, standing on plinth feet, c.1710

Fig. 48 Oak-style corner cupboard on stand, c.1720

Fig. 49 Two-tier, bow-fronted corner cupboard in walnut veneer, c.1710

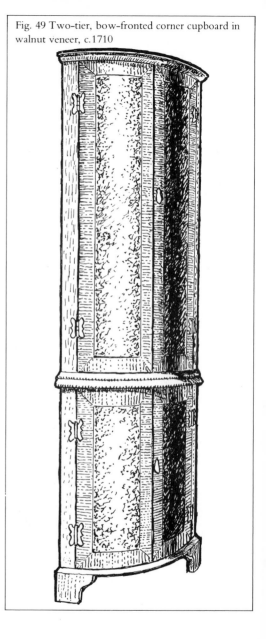

Corner cupboards came into general use around 1700, but reference is made to them in the first half of the seventeenth century. The early ones were of the hanging variety, usually with domed tops with the cornice mould following the shape of the dome. This was often crested with carving and turned and carved finials. The carcase stiles were decorated, sometimes with four or five vertical flutes, or with an applied turned half column or with carved floral drops.

A favourite finish for some of the early cabinets was lacquer, usually in the Chinese style of decoration and on these the doors were often flush-faced, not panelled, Fig. 47.

Veneered walnut cupboards usually had framed doors sometimes with a sunken panel or a fielded panel. A number of cabinets were made with mirrors in the doors instead of the wood panels, or with plain glass so that china could be displayed.

In the beginning of the eighteenth century the corner cupboard became free-standing on a three-leg base carcase, Fig. 48, or as a two-tier cupboard in the style of other cabinets of the period, Fig. 49. A number of corner cupboards were made with bow-fronts of both the hanging and the free-standing variety.

Chests were made with solid timber carcases on a base mould with bun feet. The carcase was elaborately veneered with burr or figured

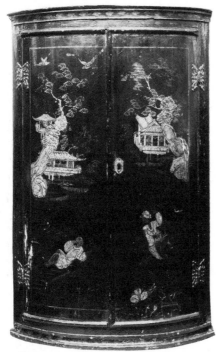

Fig. 47 Bow-fronted corner cupboard with laquer decoration, c.1770

Fig. 50 Small batchelor, flap-top chest with an overlapping ovolo mould on the drawers, c.1710

33

Fig. 51 Marquetry veneered chest of drawers on a stand with flat frame stretchers, c.1680

Fig. 52 Walnut-veneered chest of drawers on a cabriole leg stand with a double bead on the carcase round the edge of the drawers, c.1690

walnut or with marquetry panels using fruit woods and other decorative timbers on a walnut background. The hinged tops were constructed in the same manner as the cupboard doors and veneered to match the carcase. Occasionally a row of drawers was fitted into the front, bottom edge of the carcase.

Chests of drawers were now made using a solid carcase construction, with four or more full width drawers dovetailed together at all four corners. The front dovetails on the early drawers were cut through and showed on the face of the drawer front were then veneered, Fig. 92, page 50. Around 1700 the dovetails were cloaked by cutting a rebate round the front edges of the drawer and fitting a lath with an ovolo-moulded edge which overlapped on to the carcase, Fig. 92. The drawer linings were made of oak or deal. On earlier chests, a half-round or double half-round cross-band mould was fitted on the drawer rails and on the front edges of the carcase, Fig. 51 and Fig. 52.

About the beginning of the last quarter of the seventeenth century, chests of drawers were made with a separate carcase base. This was usually composed of a row of two or more drawers standing on bobbin-turned, column or spiral-twist legs on a flat frame stretcher supported by bun feet, Fig. 51. A mould was planted on the top edge of this carcase dividing it from the top carcase.

Cabinets in construction followed the style of the cupboards and the chests, usually with two separate carcases. The top carcase was fitted with doors and often the interior was lined with drawers, or alternatively it had glazed doors and shelves. The lower carcase was the same as those on the chests of drawers, Fig. 44, page 31.

Writing cabinets and bureaux
Writing cabinets from approximately 1675 were lined with drawers but instead of doors on the front they had a vertical drop-down flap which acted as the writing area. The lower carcase matched the style of the cabinets, Fig. 53 and Fig. 54.

The sloping-top bureau, dating from approximately 1690, was composed of the writing section only, supported on legs. The flap-over writing top, when open, was supported by slide-out, or gate-legs opening

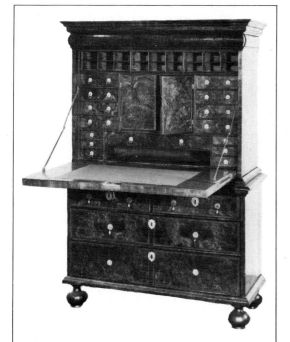

Fig. 53 Walnut-veneered writing cabinet with the writing flap open to show fitted interior, c.1700

Fig. 54 Walnut-veneered writing cabinet similar to Fig. 53, c.1700

35

from the underframe, Fig. 55. Around 1700
the carcases were made with drawers below
the writing section and were supported on legs
or bun feet to match the chests and cabinets.
The writing flap, when open, was supported
by pull-out slides which were situated on each
side of the top drawer, Fig. 56.

Wardrobes were constructed with two carcases
similar to the cabinets with doors on the
upper, and drawers in the bottom carcase.

Fig. 55 Small walnut bureau with gate-legs to support the
writing flap, c.1690

Fig. 56 Small walnut bureau with pull-out slides to
support the writing flap and drawers beneath, c.1700

Chairs

At the beginning of the walnut period chairs changed considerably in style. The cup and cover or column-turned legs, Appendix 1, Fig. G and H, were replaced with bobbin-turned, spiral-twist or scroll legs, Fig. I, J and K. The backs increased in height to support the head of the person sitting. The stretchers were usually composed of two at the side with another crossing from centre to centre making a double T form. They were either bobbin-turned or spiral-twist, not square or rectangular in section as were the earlier stretchers. In addition there was a stretcher set midway from the floor and the seat between the two front legs and the two back legs. The one between the back legs was usually turned to match the T-stretchers, but the front one sometimes varied and instead of being turned, it was a pierced, carved rail with a fretted edge approximately 10cm (4in) wide, Fig. 57 and 58, often decorated with a central carved motif with carved S-scrolls on each side of it extending outward to the legs, Fig. 59.

Fig. 57 Jacobean-style chair with padded back and seat and S-scroll legs and stretcher, c.1680

Fig. 58 Jacobean-style chair similar to Fig. 57 but with shaped headrail, c.1680

Fig. 59 Jacobean-style chair with human figure front leg supports, c.1690

Fig. 60 Jacobean chair with cane-panelled back and seat, c.1690

Fig. 61 Jacobean chair with carved vertical back splats, c.1690

The back framed panel became a separate unit, the back legs no longer acting as stiles for it, but with its own stiles and only connected with mortice and tenon joints to the legs at the head and base rails, Fig. 60. The back frame was usually pierce-carved and fretted on the outside edges, in a similar manner to the front stretcher.

Instead of upholstery or a wood panel in the back frame and seat, the new technique of

Fig. 62 Jacobean fully-upholstered wing armchair, c.1690

Fig. 64 Chairs in walnut with cabriole legs with aprons on knees, turned and shaped stretchers and solid back splat, c.1710

Fig. 63 Chair in walnut with cabriole legs, turned stretchers and pierced back splat, c.1710

Fig. 65 Chair in walnut with cabriole legs, carved knees and paw feet, c.1730

caning was introduced at this time, Fig. 60. The back legs were now turned over their full length, excluding, of course, the areas where the rail and stretcher joints came, and were topped with a finial of cup and cover shape, or with a carving of a cherub head or similar shape. As an alternative to the caned frame in the back, turned or carved vertical splats were spaced between the head and base rails, Fig. 61. Another style fitted a number of horizontal rails, usually matching the front stretcher, between the legs, in ladder-back form.

With the introduction of caning, upholstery, though still sometimes used for the seats, was not used to any great extent in the backs until the last quarter of the seventeenth century.

Around 1675, the serpentine horizontal stretcher frame with bun feet and trumpet shaped legs, was introduced for chair underframes and, about the same time, fully upholstered chairs were made with padded backs, seats and pads on the arms. Wings were also fitted on some upholstered chairs, Fig. 62. The cabriole leg, Appendix 1, Fig. L, was introduced into England about 1700. The early ones were fitted with stretchers but these were dispensed with after a very short time, Fig. 63, 64 and 65 and page 123.

Fig. 72 Walnut settee of twin-chair construction with solid back splats and ball and claw legs with scallop shell decoration on the knees, c.1720

Fig. 66 Jacobean stool with S-scroll legs and stretchers, c.1680

Fig. 68 Gilt stool (right) with human figure supports, *en suite* with Fig. 59, c.1690

Stools, couches, day-beds and settees

The underframes of all these followed the pattern of the chairs. The stools and day-beds were either caned or had padded seats, Fig. 66, 67 and 68. The head-end of the day-beds matched the chairs, the seats extending with six or eight legs to form the bed. The couches and settees repeated the designs of the chairs, but were extended in width to give seating

accommodation for two or more people, Fig. 69. The backs were either wood splats, caned, upholstered pads, or fully upholstered with or without wings, Fig. 70 and 71. The arms were wood with or without pads, or fully upholstered. Often the settee design had the appearance of two or more chairs joined together, Fig. 72.

Fig. 69 Walnut settee with cabriole legs, back panel and loose upholstered seat, c.1710

Fig. 70 Fully upholstered walnut settee with scroll arms, c.1720

Fig. 71 Walnut settee, similar to Fig. 70 but with carved ball feet, c.1720

Fig. 67 Stool in walnut with cabriole legs, aprons on the knees and square pad feet, c.1710

41

Tables

Although a small number of both rectangular and gate-leg dining tables were made in walnut, oak still seems to have been the most popular timber. The bobbin or spiral-twist legs and stretchers gradually replaced the column legs and square section stretchers of the early gate-leg tables, Fig. 32 and 33.

In side tables and occasional tables the change in design and the cabinet makers craft was far more pronounced. The tops and rails were veneered with figured or burr walnut or with marquetry, and one or more drawers were usually fitted in the front instead of the plain rail. They stood on bun-shaped feet which supported a flat frame, serpentine stretcher, and the legs were either square section, S-scrolls, spiral-twist or trumpet shape, Fig. 73, 74 and 75.

From approximately 1700 the cabriole style leg was also used, usually without understretchers, Fig. 76. Dressing-tables were made from approximately 1680. The underframes were the same style as those of the side tables, but the drawer and side rails were extended into a fretted apron with a cut away section at the front to allow for the knees of the person sitting at it, Fig. 77.

Card tables were made from approximately 1700, with a flap-over top, square or turned, trumpet-shaped legs and stretchers, usually of square section, with one or two gate-legs opening to receive the flap-top. Card tables were also made with cabriole legs with one or

Fig. 74 Side table with spiral-twist legs, bun feet and horizontal, fret-edged stretchers, c.1690

Fig. 73 Side table with S-scroll legs, bun feet and horizontal, fret-edged stretcher, c.1685

Fig. 76 Side table with ball and claw legs and aprons below the drawers, c.1700

Fig. 77 Dressing-table on pear-shaped cabriole legs, c. 1715

Fig. 75 Side table with trumpet legs, bun feet and horizontal stretcher. An apron is fitted with finials under the drawers, c.1695

43

both of the rear legs swinging out to support the flap-top when open, Fig. 78. Because these legs have no underframe and are fixed only at the rail, minus stretchers, they are usually called fly-legs.

Toilet and wall mirrors

Until about the beginning of the walnut period mirrors in England were of burnished metal, except for a small number brought over from the Continent. The Duke of Buckingham started a glass works in Vauxhall in 1663 and his method of producing the plates was to blow glass cylinders, slit and flatten them on a stone slab, and then polish the surfaces. The backs were then silvered by floating mercury over the surface and backing with tin foil. This process continued until the late eighteenth century, when a process of coating the mirror backs with pure silver was used.

Wall mirrors appear to have been made in two styles until towards the end of the seventeenth century. Either with an ornately carved frame of flowers, foliage, birds, and cherubs – usually of lime and in the style of the master carver Grinling Gibbons (1648–1721), Fig. 79, or with a walnut or marquetry veneered mould which curved from a low outside edge upwards to the mirror plate forming a cushion effect, Fig. 80. The carved frames were either painted or gilded and a small number were made with embossed silver on the face of the wood frame.

Fig. 79 Wall mirror in pine and lime made by Grinling Gibbons, c.1680

Fig. 78 Card table with ball and claw feet, carved knees and cut-outs in the top for counters. Probably made by Scottish craftsmen, c.1720

Fig. 80 Cushion wall mirror with cross-banded walnut veneer, c.1690

The cushion mirrors were usually topped with an ornately carved cresting. About 1690, the designs changed and the main plate was bordered with narrow mirror plates framed with small carved moulds, Fig. 81. These border plates were often decorated on the back with gold, silver and colours, *verre eglomisé*, Fig. 82. The top cresting was usually of shaped mirror plates enclosed in carvings and all the woodwork was usually given a gilt finish. Towards the end of the Queen Anne period (1702–1714), the mirror frames were composed of a small ogee mould 25–36mm (1–1½in) with a carved cresting and an apron at the bottom with scroll-fretted edges, Fig. 83. A common decoration for the top centre of the cresting was a carved scallop shell. The whole of the frame was usually gilded but, on some of the very late ones, the moulds were cross-banded walnut and the cresting and aprons were left plain on the face and veneered with walnut, with fretted edges.

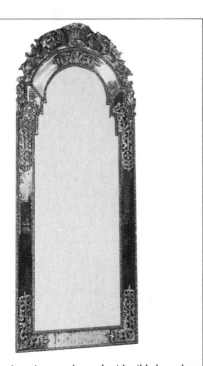

Fig. 81 Wall mirror in carved wood with gilded overlays on glass border, c.1700

Fig. 83 Wall mirror with gilt and walnut-grained mould and gilded aprons, c.1720

Fig. 82 Wall mirror with a carved and gilded and *verre eglomisé* decoration on the glass borders, c.1700

Toilet mirrors were usually made with a drawer-lined carcase base. Some had flap lids similar to the sloping-top bureaux; others were elaborately serpentine shaped on the front both in the width and height. Square-section standards, usually topped with a turned finial, supported the pivoting mirror frame which was a small copy of the later wall mirrors, excluding the bottom apron, and often the top cresting too. The mirror plates were usually bevelled and the top edges cut in various serpentine shapes and the frame mould was cut and shaped to match, Fig. 84. Most of these toilet mirrors were made in walnut, but some were parcel-gilded and others were lacquered and decorated in the Chinese manner, Fig. 85.

Beds

About the time of the Restoration beds became even more elaborate. The canopy or tester was retained, but the cornice moulds were either carved, and decorated with gold leaf as were the crestings and finials at the corners, or they were upholstered with ornate needlework covers and tassel or braid trimming, Fig. 86. The tester was not always supported by posts at the foot end, some were suspended by bars from the ceiling. Curtains were still drawn to fully enclose the occupants.

Timber

Although this was the period when walnut was the popular show wood, other woods were used for the mainly unseen construction work. Oak and deal, a general term for any softwood, were used for cabinet construction to be veneered over with walnut. Yew was also cut for veneers. Oak, ash, beech, chestnut, birch and deal were used for chair making under gilded, painted or lacquer finishes, and also for bed rails and under upholstery.

Decoration

The walnut furniture depended mainly on the cabinet makers arrangement of the figured grain, burrs and inlays in decorative designs and form to get the maximum beauty from the grain of the wood itself, but gold was sometimes used on walnut furniture to enhance carvings and moulds.

Oil gilding and water gilding   Gilding was used on English furniture from the Middle Ages but it was only in the last quarter of the seventeenth century that it became really popular. Oil gilding was the process used mainly at this period. The surfaces to be gilded were brush coated with a gesso solution

Fig. 84 Walnut toilet mirror with bureau-style base, c.1710

Fig. 85 Lacquered toilet mirror with bureau-style base, c.1700

46

Fig. 86 Upholstered bed with needlework trimmings on headboard and tester. The carvings are gilt and in the centre of the cornice section is the cypher of James II, c.1687

composed of whitening, glue size, and a small amount of vegetable oil which made it easier to apply. The gesso was mixed to a creamy consistency and several coats were applied and left to harden. The surface was then rubbed down thoroughly until it was smooth and even and any loose pigment was then removed with a damp cloth. The oil size, coloured with pigment, was then brushed evenly over the surface. The early craftsmen seem to have had a preference for a yellow pigment in the size but red, brown or pink was also used. The size was left until it was almost dry, before the gold leaf, which was approximately in 75mm (3in) squares, was applied.

Water gilded furniture has the same gesso surface preparation. This is followed by applying parchment size and red clay, called bole, mixed to a creamy consistency with hot water, to the surface. When it has completely hardened it is smoothed in the same way as the gesso. The gold leaf is cut to a size convenient for whatever shape is being gilded. This is done by laying the gold leaf on a gilder's cushion, a padded board covered with suede, using a knife designed for the purpose. Water is spread over the surface of the wood to be gilded and the gold leaf is laid on to it using a brush known as a gilder's tip, Fig. 87.

Gilding was used in various ways; some furniture was completely covered with gold and cabinets decorated in this way were usually made of softwood such as pine and the chairs were usually made of beech or a similar wood. An alternative was to paint the piece of

Fig. 87 Gilder's cushion, knife and tip (top left)
Fig. 88 The marquetry cutter's donkey being used by Peter Mactaggart (bottom left)
Fig. 89 Long-case clock decorated with marquetry, c.1690

furniture and to gild only the carved decoration, parcel gilding, and a third was to polish a piece of walnut furniture and to gild only the carving.

Lacquer Lacquered furniture had various background colours including green, red, gold and black on to which decorative designs, usually in the Chinese style, were gilded or painted. A process called 'bantam work' was also used. This was a method of carving and building up the lacquer in relief, and the lacquer for this process was usually confined to one colour.

Marquetry This was a process where light coloured wood veneers such as apple, pear and sycamore were glued face to face, with a layer of paper between each face, to a background veneer of walnut. The paper ensured that they could easily be separated again. A paper pattern of the design was glued on top of the layer of veneers, which were clamped on the 'donkey', the name given to the marquetry cutter's bench and vice, Fig. 88. The floral, foliage and geometrical designs were then cut with the fine fret-saw. After cutting, the veneers were separated and the panels made up into a complete design. The floral, foliage and geometrical shapes of the background walnut veneer were discarded and replaced with shapes from the other veneers, Fig. 89. Other woods including rosewood, kingwood, coromandel and laburnum were used when more colourful marquetry was desired. Shading on floral veneers was achieved by dipping them in hot sand.

moulds planted round the inside front edge of the frames which hung over to form a rebate and the glass panels were divided up into rectangular shapes by moulds of the same shape, Fig. 95. From the beginning of the eighteenth century tracery in the doors of cabinets became much more delicate, mainly astragal-shaped but a large half-section oval was also to be seen on the doors of the early cabinets. At this time, too, tracery designs became much more elaborate and instead of just rectangular panels, included curved work.

With the coming of solid construction all joints were glued instead of being fixed with wood or metal pins as they were with frame and panel construction. Towards the end of the seventeenth century, dowel jointing instead of mortice and tenon was used on some chair headrails or occasionally for fixing stands to carcases. Cornice friezes were usually curved cushion shape, in the William and Mary period, Fig. 53, page 35, but this appears to have gone out of favour by the beginning of the eighteenth century to be replaced by a flat frieze.

Fittings   The ornamental plate face fixing hinges were still in use through this period, Fig. 43, page 29. Butt hinges were used occasionally, but it was not until around 1760 that they came into general use. They were fixed on the edge of the door or carcase in such a way that only the butt showed when the door was closed.

Brass pins were still in use for fixing fittings,

Fig. 95 Small walnut cabinet with square tracery in the glazed door, c.1730

but around the beginning of the period brass screws started to be used. The earliest ones were completely made by hand and had a parallel shank, and it was not until approximately 1760 that they were turned on a lathe and were not pointed or tapered.

Early handles, up to about 1700, were usually of pear-drop or similar shape, Fig. 96, but later

Fig. 96 Period handles
Fig. 97 Period escutcheons

the loop grip with swan neck ends on a fretted and sometimes pierced or engraved back-plate, were made in brass. These were fixed with two bolts, their round heads bored to receive the pins of the grip, which passed through the back plate and through the drawer front and were fixed with a nut at the back. On a small number of the very early handles a split pin was used instead of the bolts.

51

Polishing and finishing There was no change in the materials used in this period from those in the earlier one, except that hot beeswax was used on walnut to enhance the colour. Lacquer was in use for furniture during most of the seventeenth century but was mostly imported. It was not until the end of the century that the English method came into general use. For this the wood surface was prepared with gesso and this was coated with pigmented varnish, usually black, and then decorated with Chinese floral decorations.

Walnut oystershell cabinet on stand c.1690

Fig. 98 Mahogany cabinet with framed, fielded panels in framed doors and carving on cornice, belly mould and plinth, c.1750

The Georgian period 1714-1830

Robert Adam 1728–1792;   Thomas Chippendale 1718–1779;
Thomas Chippendale Jnr. 1749–1822;
George Hepplewhite died 1786;   William Kent 1686–1748;
Thomas Sheraton 1751–1806;   Thomas Hope 1769–1831

The beginning of this period could also be referred to as the start of the mahogany period, starting approximately in 1720, when a shortage of walnut caused the furniture makers to look to other parts of the world for supplies of suitable timber.

Cupboards, cabinets, wardrobes and bureaux

The early mahogany cupboards were of solid construction, not veneered, so ornamentation was achieved by reverting back to frame and panel construction for the doors, usually with fielded panels and carved moulds which were either planted or worked on the inside edges of the frames surrounding the panels. Planted moulds are separate moulds not worked on stiles or rails. Frieze moulds and sections of the cornice mould were also carved, as was the belly mould dividing the upper carcase from the lower one, Fig. 98.

A new feature used on the cornice was the broken pediment, Fig. 99. This consisted of

Fig. 99 An example of a broken pediment on cabinet cornice, c.1740

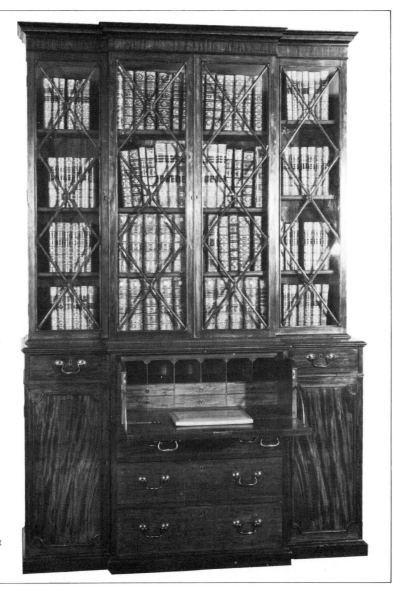

Fig. 100 Mahogany break-front bookcase with pull-out drawer drop-front secretaire, c. 1780

two sections of cornice mould planted on top of the main cornice, rising from the front outside edge of the cornice at an angle of about forty degrees towards the centre of the cabinet, but not meeting. The area within the angles is filled with a flat frieze board, fretted on the upper edge between the two moulds. This architectural style was a feature of early mahogany furniture, another example being carved corbels on the pilasters under the cornice. This was due to the influence of designers like William Kent who were primarily architects rather than furniture designers. There was a further development in the cornice pediment around 1760, the canted moulds, instead of being straight, were now ogee-shaped, usually called swan-neck, Fig. 101, in length. The bases of the early cupboards were either solid plinths, Fig. 100, or were fretted plinth feet, Fig. 101, but around 1750 these were superseded by the ogee-moulded plinth foot, Fig. 102, or by the cabriole leg, both of which were often elaborately carved.

Early in the second half of the eighteenth century the lower carcase of some of the more expensive cupboards were ogee-shaped on the front and ends, or bombe-shaped as it is usually called.

Veneer came into fairly general use again in the second half of the eighteenth century, when the mahogany from which curls and fiddleback veneers could be selected and cut was imported, and this resulted in a reduction of carving, as it did in the walnut period.

Fig. 101 Mahogany cabinet with astragal-moulded tracery
doors and plinth feet, c.1760

Fig. 102 Mahogany wardrobe with full-length hanging
space and ogee feet, c.1760

Fig. 103 Satinwood cabinet with marble mosaic inlays, marquetry and ormolu mounts, c.1770

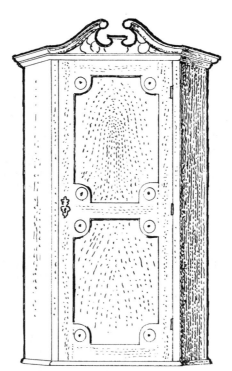

Fig. 104 Mahogany corner cupboard with a swan-neck pediment, c.1760

With the introduction of veneering again, fruit wood, boxwood and other light coloured woods were used with mahogany for banding and inlay decoration. A small number of cupboards were made in solid mahogany and veneered with satinwood. These were usually fairly plain in construction but elaborately ornamented with inlays of various woods, mainly in classical designs, Fig. 103, or alternatively had a painted floral decoration. Robert Adam, who favoured painted furniture, made cupboards in pine with applied classical carvings such as urns, rosettes and floral drapes. The cupboards were painted cream, or pastel shades of blue or green, and the carved decoration was either gilded or painted in a different colour.

Corner cupboards in mahogany varied little from those of the walnut period, except for the cornice pediments which were usually swan-neck, Fig. 104. One innovation which became popular towards the end of the first quarter of the eighteenth century was the tracery door. Instead of the solid wood panel or plain glass doors, the panel area was divided by a double-rebated moulding into smaller panels which were glazed separately. The most popular of these is probably the fifteen pattern. The cupboards were still made in the hanging and free-standing styles, but in the latter part of the period, the base was a cupboard instead of just a stand as in earlier designs shown in Fig. 49 and 50, page 32-3. Cabinets of the Georgian period matched in style and design the cupboards of the period, but their interiors were either completely lined with small drawers and cupboards enclosed by wood panelled doors, or with shelves and glazed doors for displaying china. The china cabinets were made on a stand or separate cupboard, or stood on a chest of drawers, which brought the glazed section to eye level, and the doors were usually tracery worked, Fig. 105. Bookcases became popular at the beginning of this period. The early ones were similar in style to the china cabinets, Fig. 101, page 55, but around 1750 the break-front bookcase superseded these, Fig. 106. They were made

Fig. 105 Mahogany cabinet with a swan-neck pediment,
c.1760

Fig. 106 Break-front bookcase decorated with marquetry
and with carved tracery in the glazed doors, c.1770

Fig. 107 Mahogany wardrobe with drawers in the lower carcase and curl veneers used on the door panels, c.1760

Fig. 108 Mahogany bureau-bookcase with mirror panel doors and ogee feet, c.1765

Fig. 109 Edwardian davenport, c.1900

up of three main carcases standing side by side, the centre section approximately double the width of the other sections and greater in depth by about 15cm (6in). The bookcase sections stood on separate carcases fitted with drawers and cupboards although some were fitted with a writing area in the centre section, Fig. 100, page 54.

Wardrobes in this period were still made with two carcases as they were in the walnut period, but around the mid-eighteenth century, instead

Fig. 110 Mahogany multi-gateleg dining table, c.1760

of the bottom carcase being fitted with a single row of drawers, it was now two or three drawers in height and the upper cupboard section was fitted with pull-out trays, Fig. 107.

Bureaux were still very similar in design to those of the late walnut period, the main variation being the style of the feet, and the decoration, Fig. 108.

Another piece of furniture which became popular around 1800 was the sloping-top writing desk. This was composed of a pedestal of drawers or a cupboard, usually showing false drawers in the ends. The writing area, which slightly sloped towards the writer, was also the lid to a fitted box compartment fixed on top of the pedestal. Behind the writing area was a further lidded box compartment which was fitted to contain ink bottles, pens, etc. On some of these desks the sloping writing box was made to slide forward over the knees of the writer; on others the pedestal was narrow and two turned or cabriole-shaped legs

supported the front of the writing section, Fig. 109. This type of desk is called a davenport, probably because records show that a desk of this kind was supplied by Gillows to a Captain Davenport.

Dining tables were still in the gate-leg style, but from around 1760 two separate D-shaped tables, which could be used as side-tables, were made, Fig. 110 and 111 and these were clipped to the main table to extend the length. Later in this period, dining tables were made in three

59

Fig. 111 Mahogany multi-gateleg dining table with
D-ends supported by centre columns, c.1780

Fig. 112 Dining table with separate sections supported by
centre columns, c.1800

Fig. 113 Mahogany sofa table with centre support, c.1800

Fig. 114 Mahogany sofa table with end supports, c.1800

or more separate sections, usually on column and splayed legs, Fig. 112. These sections, together with extra loose leaves, could be connected together with clips to make the table to any size required.

Sofa tables were made in the later part of this period. They were approximately 120cm (4ft) long and extending to about 180cm (6ft) when the end leaves were raised. The leaves were supported by folding wooden brackets. There are a number of variations in design for these tables. Some had a centre column with four splay leg supports, Fig. 113; some had four columns and a base block supported by splay legs, while others had four square legs cut in an exaggerated ogee shape, connected by a circular block about a foot above ground level. The most sought-after sofa tables today are those with lyre-shaped end supports and splay legs, connected together with a stretcher which is usually turned. The end support type are also shown with panel ends, Fig. 104, or with column or multi-columns at the ends and splay legs.

In the last quarter of the eighteenth century, drum, rent or library tables were made. These were usually round or octagonal in shape with a row of drawers round the under edge of the top, and supported on either a column and splay legs, Fig. 115 or a box carcase, Fig. 116.

Also in the second half of the century the nest of tables, which were graduated in size to be fitted inside each other, was made, usually in sets of four.

Fig. 115 Mahogany drum or library table, c.1800

Fig. 116 Mahogany and satinwood rent table, c.1800

Fig. 117 Gilded chair in the style of William Kent, c.1730

Fig. 119 Gilded settee by William Kent, c.1730

Fig. 118 Gilded scissor-leg stool by Henry Williams in the Kent style, c.1740

The designs of William Kent (1686–1748)

All the cabinets, cupboards and bookcases in the style of William Kent have an architectural appearance, with heavy broken cornices, deep carved pilasters and moulds and solid plinth bases, Fig. 98, page 53. The amount of carved ornament gives an almost clumsy appearance to his furniture and most of the furniture is either painted or gilded.

Chairs and stools, like his cabinets, were liberally ornamented with heavy carving on the backs, arms, legs and rails, Fig. 117 and 118. Carved aprons were often hung from the underside of the rails and crestings, carved in the same manner, were planted on top of the head rail. The legs, cabriole in style, had ball and claw, lion paw or scroll feet. Seat sizes were of generous proportions. His settees like his other furniture were heavily ornamented with carving which complicated the construction, Fig. 119.

Fig. 121 Gilded side table with scroll legs in the style of Kent, c.1730

Fig. 122 Gilt wall mirror in the style of Chippendale, c.1750

Fig. 120 Gilded side table with pillar legs in the style of Kent, c.1730

Tables by Kent usually had marble or scagliola (a composition of lime, marble, brick, etc.) tops, the rails and legs were ornately carved and pierced and carved aprons were often fixed on the underside of the rails, Fig. 120 and 121.

Beds by Kent were in the style of the late walnut period.

Mirrors designed by Kent and Chippendale are so similar that, unless they are authenticated by an account or something similar, it is almost impossible to be sure which of the two was responsible. Some frames were elaborately carved and pierced and usually gilded or paint and parcel gilded, Fig. 122 and 123, others were made with a narrow mould surrounding the glass which could either be gilded, mahogany or mahogany and parcel-gilt, Fig. 124. A cresting and apron, usually cross-banded with mahogany veneer or gilded, was fitted to the top and bottom moulds and

Fig. 123 Gilded wall mirror in Chinese Chippendale style, c.1760

Fig. 124 Walnut wall mirror with aprons and carved and gilded decoration on the crest and sides, c.1720

Fig. 125 Walnut wall mirror with a gilded bird carving on crest, c.1720

usually extended partly on to the side moulds. The outside edges were fretted normally in scroll shapes, Fig. 125. A scallop shell or eagle with spread wings was often planted on the cresting.

Decoration
William Kent was obviously a great lover of carving and his designs, particularly for chairs and tables are excessively decorated. The scallop shell was one of his favourite

decorations, Fig. 126, others were animal and human masks and figures, the acanthus leaf, ornate floral drops and festoons. The mouldings, like his carvings, were in high relief and they too were carved with acanthus, egg and dart, or similar designs. Cornices were massive, usually with the broken pediment, Fig. 99, page 53, and carved floral ornament decorated pilasters and corbels on cabinets and fireplace surrounds. His chairs were carved in high relief on all available show-wood

Fig. 126 An example of the scallop shell decoration

65

Fig. 127 Mahogany commode by William Vile in the style of Chippendale, c.1750

Fig. 128 Gilded bombe-shaped chest, c.1725

surfaces, Fig. 117, page 63, legs were cabriole style with masks or acanthus leaf on the front knees, and with scroll, lions paw or ball and claw feet, Appendix 1. Tables, too, were ornately carved with flower, fruit and mask decoration in high relief, with matching carved and pierced aprons hung from the underside of the rails, Fig. 120. Mirrors were in his architectural style usually with a scallop shell pediment.

The designs of Thomas Chippendale (1718–1789)

The cabinets, cupboards and bookcases designed by Chippendale show that he, too, had a love for carving, but in a less flamboyant manner than that of Kent, and certainly the architectural appearance was not so pronounced, Fig. 127. His designs can be divided into three different styles – rococo, Gothic and Chinese. Although Chippendale is probably best known for his chair designs, his cabinets and commodes are of particular interest because of the amount of bombe-shaping in them, Fig. 128, which made it necessary for the craftsmen to use a laminated form of construction using the principle of block and laminboard of today. Chippendale bookcases are similar to those of Kent, usually of a design with architectural features, Fig. 99, page 53.

Chairs by Chippendale varied considerably in style. Between approximately 1710 and 1730 a

Fig. 129 Plain mahogany chair in the style of Chippendale, c.1750

Fig. 130 Mahogany chair with scroll ribbon decoration on splat and ball and claw legs, c.1750

Fig. 131 Mahogany chair with rose and ribbon carving on the back and carved scroll feet, c.1755

number of chairs were made with solid back splats with only the outside edges cut in various shapes, Fig. 65, page 39. These chairs were made in both mahogany and walnut but Chippendale was probably one of the first designers to show an English dining chair with a pierced back splat, although later a large number of chairs with this feature were copied by craftsmen. Some were fairly plain in design with no carving, square front legs, and double-T stretchers, the fretted splat being the only decorative feature, Fig. 129. The splat was fixed between the back seat rail and the head rail and on top of the seat rail and fitted round the front and edges of the splat was a concave moulded block called a shoe, which covered the raw back edge of the seat upholstery tacked to the rail. Sheraton, Hepplewhite and Adam appear to have preferred to put a separate rail an inch or two above the seat to receive the splat instead of using the shoe method.

A further development which Chippendale used on his dining chairs was for the splat to be carved in a loop-ribbon design, Fig. 130. The more elaborate chairs were carved with rosettes, acanthus leaf, scrolls and more intricate ribbon carvings, Fig. 131. The front legs of these chairs were usually cabriole-shaped with either lion paw, ball and claw or scroll feet, and acanthus leaf or similar carving on the knees. If the upholstered seat was the loose, drop-in type, the mould enclosing it was

Fig. 132 Mahogany ladder-back chair, c.1770

Fig. 133 Mahogany corner or library chair, c.1730

Fig. 134 Mahogany chair in gothic Chippendale style, c.1765

also carved with ball and sausage, egg and dart, gadrooning, rose and ribbon, or similar decoration. He also designed chairs with a number of carved horizontal rails in the back known as ladder-back, Fig. 132, and chairs to fit in the corner of a room, Fig. 133. The Gothic influence in his dining chairs took the form of square front legs with the faces carved to give the appearance of applied frets, Fig. 134. Pierced and shaped brackets were planted in the corners where the rail and leg

met and these chairs usually had pierce-fretted, double-T section stretcher rails. The Chinese influence in his dining chairs is shown by head rails worked and carved in a pagoda roof shape, Fig. 135, the lattice-filled back, again usually with pagoda shapes in it, and the legs either square with fretted facings similar to the Gothic, or turned imitating bamboo.

The arms of his carver chairs were usually ogee in shape as were the uprights, and the top

front edge was carved in a scroll or similar form. The backs of the upholstered chairs of Chippendale varied in three ways. The upholstery either enclosed the woodwork completely, Fig. 117, or a carved and shaped head rail and side rails framed the upholstery which fitted close to the seat upholstery, Fig. 136, or a carved rail was fitted 50–100mm (2–4in) above the seat rail and the upholstery was fixed in panel form between this, the head rail and the side rails, Fig. 137.

Fig. 135 Chair in Chinese Chippendale style, c.1760

Fig. 136 Gilded hair in the style of Chippendale, c.1750

Fig. 137 Mahogany and parcel-gilt chair in the style of Kent or Chippendale, c.1750

Stools by Chippendale repeated in style the legs and underframes of the chairs, Fig. 138. They were made with three, four or more legs.

He also designed stools with scissor legs similar to those in Fig. 118, page 63. Settees, like those from the walnut period, repeated the style of the chairs, Fig. 139 and often gave the appearance of two or more chairs joined together.

Fig. 138 Gilded stool with cabriole and scroll legs in the style of Chippendale, *en suite* with Fig. 136, c.1750

69

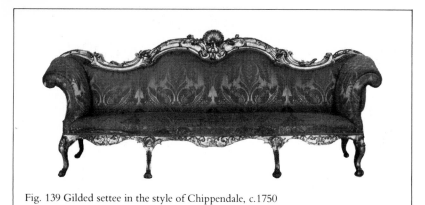

Fig. 139 Gilded settee in the style of Chippendale, c.1750

Fig. 140 Gilded side table with cabriole and scroll legs in the style of Chippendale, c.1730

Fig. 142 Mahogany side table with open fret and carved legs, c.1760

Fig. 141 Mahogany side table with cluster column legs in the style of Chippendale, c.1760

Dining tables of the early Chippendale period were mainly gate-legged, square or rectangular in shape and supported on square or turned legs. By having two or more extra sections they could be clipped together to form one large table, Fig. 110. Gate-leg dining tables in this period were also made round or oval shape with cabriole legs and the gates pivoted with wooden knuckle or finger joints instead of the metal hinge or wood pin pivot.

Side tables of the Chippendale period were similar to those designed by Kent but the carving, though used extensively, was not quite so overpowering, Fig. 140. Chippendale also designed tables with cluster column, Fig. 141, and open fret legs, Fig. 142. A number of these tables were gilded, others were of polished mahogany or parcel-gilt, Fig. 143.

Occasional tables were designed for various purposes. Tea tables with four legs had two leaves supported by brackets which folded on to the rails when not in use, this is known as the Pembroke style. A number of these tables were designed with an open-fret box structure fitted under the rails which was used to store the prepared food until it was to be eaten, Fig. 144.

Silver or china tables usually rectangular in shape and delicate in construction were designed with four legs usually of cluster column or open-fretted style; the top was rectangular or serpentine edged with a raised, open-fretted rim, Fig. 145.

Fig. 143 Parcel-gilt table with ball and claw feet and carved aprons, c.1750

Fig. 144 Pembroke table with brass grilles enclosing the food shelf, c.1770

Fig. 145 Silver table with cluster column legs, c.1760

Tripod tables on cabriole splay legs and turned column were designed with a variety of shaped tops; some were square with open-fretted rims similar to the silver tables, Fig. 146, others had a raised carved rim, Fig. 147. Some were round with a raised moulded rim on the outside top edge and others were scalloped round the edge with a raised moulded pie-crust rim, Fig. 148. Most of the tops were made to tip up when not in use, but on some the top was made to spin round by having a box-like section fixed under the top and a wedge passing through the column on the top side of the box-base as shown in Fig. 147. Card tables were designed with flap tops and gate or fly legs. Alternatively the end rails had a folding extension which opened in concertina-fashion when the back legs were drawn out, showing rails going completely round the underside of the top. The more elaborate tables were serpentine-shaped or had semi-circular corners with a circular routed-out area in each corner of the opened top in which to place the money or counters, Fig. 78, page 44.

Beds designed by Chippendale were similar to those of the late walnut period and those by Kent, but probably less festooned with material and certainly showing the rococo, Gothic or Chinese influence, Fig. 149.

Decoration

Thomas Chippendale used carving very much in the same way as Kent but his was low relief and more restrained. He favoured acanthus leaf decoration, Fig. 150 and the egg and dart and similar carving on mouldings but he particularly favoured rose and ribbon carving which he used on his high quality furniture, Fig. 151. Cornices by Chippendale were ornate with Chinese or Gothic influence or alternatively with the swan-neck pediments carved with rosettes or acanthus leaf on the scroll-ends Fig. 101, page 55. The area between the swan-necks was sometimes filled with a fretted or carved panel. The friezes on the cornice were usually fret decorated or carved and, like Kent, he also used the broken pediment cornice, Fig. 99, page 53.

On his main cornice mould above the frieze he also shows dental, Greek key, Fig. 152, and ball and sausage bead decoration.

He used the cabriole leg with various feet but on the knees he seems to have preferred the acanthus leaf rather than the masks favoured by Kent. Mirrors and picture frames of Chippendale style were ornamented with acanthus leaves and scrolls. He appears to have used the C-scroll in abundance, Fig. 153, maybe because it is the initial of his name! On cabinets he also used both cabriole and plinth types of feet, and of the plinth feet he obviously favoured the ogee-moulded, Appendix 1, page 120. His bookcases and glass-panelled cabinets have a large variety of tracery in the doors, Fig. 105, page 57.

Fig. 149 Mahogany bed with gadrooning and acanthus leaf carving on cornice, c.1750

Fig. 150 An example of
acanthus leaf decoration

Fig. 151 An example of rose and ribbon carving

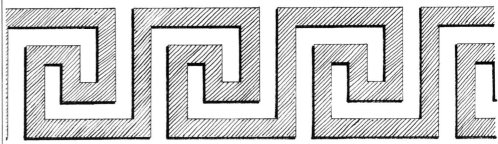

Fig. 152 An example of greek key decoration

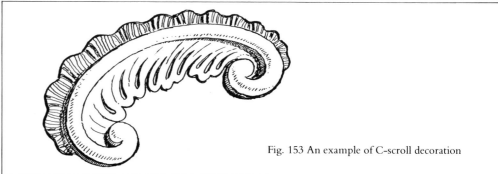

Fig. 153 An example of C-scroll decoration

Fig. 154 Painted pedestal with carved decoration in the style of Adam, c.1775

Fig. 155 Mahogany pedestal cupboard surmounted by an urn, c.1780

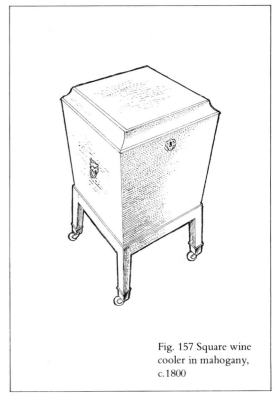
Fig. 157 Square wine cooler in mahogany, c.1800

The designs of Robert Adam (1728–1792)

There is no doubt that Adam was responsible for the classical revival in England and this is shown in his furniture designs, Fig. 154, and even more pronounced in the decoration of his room interiors. He undoubtedly influenced the other furniture designers in the second half of the eighteenth century. The cabinets, cupboards and bookcases by Adam were delicate and simple in construction, square or turned legs replaced the previously popular cabriole style. The friezes, rails and other flat surfaces were decorated either with delicate, intricate applied carving, wood inlays or paint using designs of Greek or Roman origin, Fig. 103, page 56.

Adam sideboards are particularly interesting, being composed of a central table with drawers or cupboards, and pedestal cupboards at each side of it surmounted by wood urns, Fig. 155. A wine cooler was often made to match and fit under the sideboard, Fig. 156 and 157. His commodes, half-round in shape, were simple cupboards intricately decorated with carving, inlay or paint, Fig. 158. Chairs by Adam were simple in design with mainly turned or square front legs often with a spade-shaped foot, referred to by the furniture trade as the Adam toe, Appendix I, page 120.

Fig. 158 Bow-fronted satinwood commode with coloured floral decoration on top, c.1780

Fig. 156 Oval wine cooler with satinwood decoration, c.1780

Fig. 159 Carved and painted armchair designed by Adam, *en suite* with Fig. 163 and 164, c.1775

The backs of his chairs were a simple oval or square shape with an upholstered panel, Fig. 159, or with decorated horizontal rails or vertical splats, Fig. 160. The legs, rails, backs and arms were decorated with delicate carving and painted, Fig. 162 or polished, or had painted decoration, Fig. 161

Stools, too, were of simple construction with upholstered seats, often with scroll-shaped arm rests, Fig. 163. Settees had serpentine head rails and open arms or scroll-shaped arms like the stools, Fig. 164. Tables designed by Adam were also simple their attraction being mainly in the decoration which was in the classic style, Fig. 165 and 166.

revival in English furniture decoration and this included fine delicate carving of urns, rams' heads, floral festoons and scrolls, Fig. 168. A favourite motif which he used in various ways was the husk, often called the Adam husk in the furniture trade, Fig. 169.

These motifs were also designed for coloured wood inlay, painting or marble mosaic. The cornices of his cabinets, though fairly plain in construction, were ornamented with carving or inlay and with pediments of urns, figures, etc., and the pilasters were mainly flat with carved or inlaid decoration. His designs for feet and legs were mainly square-tapered, with or without a foot, or turned on a lathe, Appendix 1, page 120. They were often decorated with a rosette on the top square with a series of tapering husks, or similar, down to the foot. Fluting and reeding on legs, friezes, etc., are also common in Adam designs and Greek key and honeysuckle decoration, Fig. 200, page 96, is also shown on friezes.

The sabre leg is used in some of his chair designs, Appendix 1, page 120, although the legs are square they are shown without stretchers or underframes of any sort. His chair backs were fairly plain, either square or oval in construction, with delicate moulds or carvings on their show-wood faces. The construction of his chairs, though sturdy had not the heavy over-ornate appearance of Kent's and Chippendale's rococo styles.

Fig. 167 Overmantle mirror in the style of Adam, c.1775

Fig. 168 Examples of urn, ram's head and floral festoon decorations

Fig. 169 Examples of husk and ribbon festoon decorations

Fig. 174 Mahogany chairs with carved material draping and wheatears in the splat, c.1790

Fig. 176 Mahogany shield-back chair with carving and inlay in the triple splat, c.1790

Wardrobes and bookcases were designed with elaborate but delicate cornices, domed with carved or inlaid friezes surmounted by urns or other shaped pediments or flat with ornate swan-neck pediments surmounted by urn or other finials. Doors of frame and panel construction were veneered with curl, flame or fiddleback veneers, or inlaid. Drawer fronts were treated in the same manner. The glazed doors of the bookcases were designed with delicate tracery in the panels, Fig. 171. His

designs for pedestal cupboards were almost identical to Sheraton's and his sideboards were much the same in design as those of Adam and Sheraton, with perhaps more use made of colour and wood inlaying.

Side tables, tea tables, card and Pembroke table designs, Fig. 172 and 173 were like those of Adam and Sheraton with decorative inlays similar to the tops of the chests and commodes.

Hepplewhite chairs were more decorative than those by Adam. He copied both the simple square construction of the back, Fig. 174 and also the oval shape, but he really excelled in his shield-shaped backs, Fig. 176. He also designed wing easy chairs.

Fig. 177 Mahogany settee with carved rosette and bead decoration, c.1790

Fig. 178 Settee with show wood multi-heart shaped back, c.1800

Settee designs by Hepplewhite show the serpentine backs and scroll or open arms very much like those of Adam, Fig. 177. He also designed settees with show-wood backs of multiple chair shapes in the style of Chippendale but with a more delicate construction, often using the shield-shape, Fig. 178.

Wall mirror designs were much the same as those of Adam but, like Sheraton, he designed a large number of toilet mirrors. These were oval, shield or rectangular-shaped, pivoting between uprights and fixed on boxes, small nests of drawers, or just on splay legs. They were often inlaid with decorative coloured woods, Fig. 179.

Beds designed by Hepplewhite were of the two poster style with the draped headboard holding up the canopy or tester. The lower section of the posts at the foot end were either square pedestal style with a plinth or spade leg shape and the upper section was delicately turned and carved.

Decoration
Hepplewhite decoration is very much in the classical style of his contemporaries but, because his furniture designs were on the whole, delicate, his decoration was the same. He certainly favoured inlaying but also shows carving. He used the acanthus leaf, flower, material and husk festoons in a much more refined way. He also used rams' heads, urn shapes, rosettes and honeysuckle, but he is, perhaps, best associated with the decoration

known as the Prince of Wales feathers, Fig. 180. Reeded and fluted ornamentation was used on legs and friezes in much the same way as by Adam, and the dental, Greek key, and ball and sausage bead used by Sheraton and Chippendale, Fig. 181.

Fig. 180 An example of Prince of Wales feathers decoration

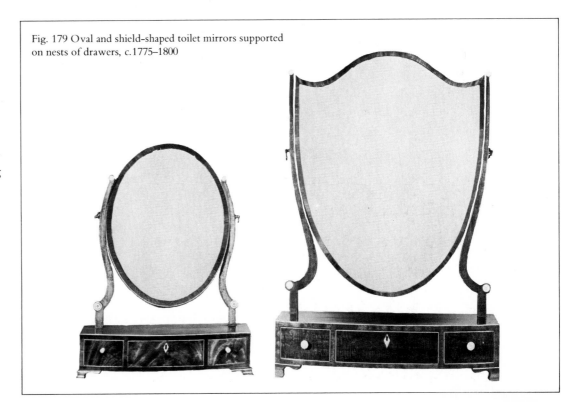

Fig. 179 Oval and shield-shaped toilet mirrors supported on nests of drawers, c.1775–1800

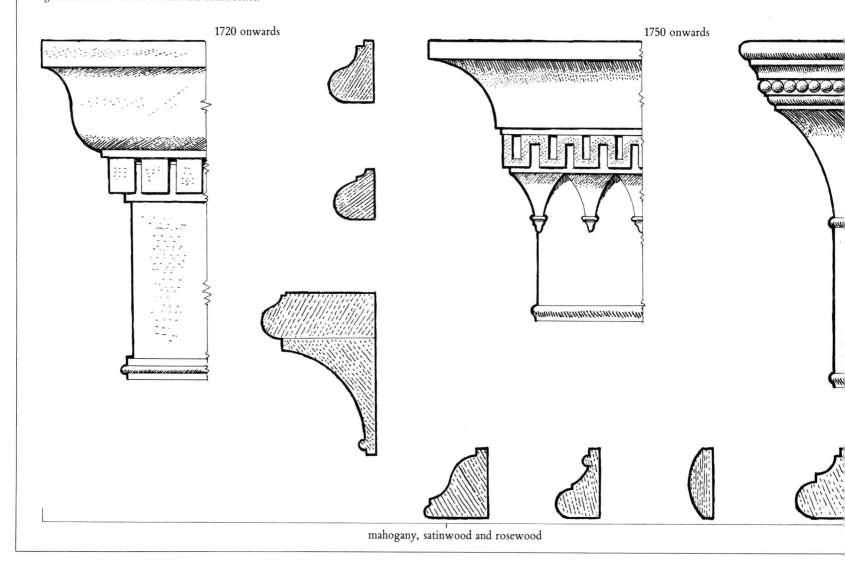

Fig. 181 Oak and walnut moulds and construction

1720 onwards

1750 onwards

mahogany, satinwood and rosewood

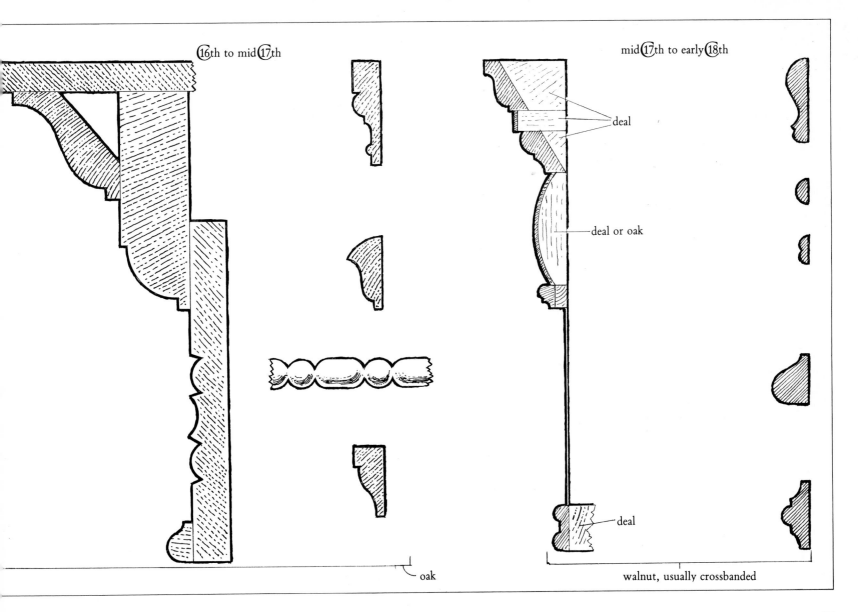

16th to mid 17th

mid 17th to early 18th

deal

deal or oak

deal

oak

walnut, usually crossbanded

87

The designs of Thomas Sheraton (1751–1806)

In his designs, Sheraton appears to have had a preference for carving and decorative veneers rather than for inlaid decoration. A large number of his designs show that either inlay or carving could be used for the decoration although his designs for decorated tops were, of course, intended for inlaying.

Chests of drawers, cupboards, cabinets and commodes designed by Sheraton were similar in construction and style to those of Adam and Hepplewhite. His chests of drawers were either square, bow or serpentine-fronted, standing on turned or square feet, often with the spade shaping, Fig. 182. He obviously favoured the splay foot, which is a delicate plinth foot with an extended toe also used by Hepplewhite and these feet are used on a large number of his chests, commodes and cupboards. Instead of the normal width rail above drawers or doors under the top of his cupboards, chests and commodes, he often shows a wider frieze rail which is usually decorated with carving or inlay.

Sideboards by Sheraton were usually serpentine or bow-fronted with flat tops, but he did design some with pedestal end cupboards and others with a brass rod gallery round the top, Fig. 183. There are also signs

Fig. 182 Mahogany-veneered chest of drawers with serpentine front, c.1775

that some of his designs were influenced by the French styles of Louis XVI.

Chair designs by Sheraton were delicate and ornate like Hepplewhite with square or serpentine-shaped head rails on moulded or turned uprights, or with shield-shaped backs, Fig. 175. The arms of his carver chairs show a

Fig. 183 Mahogany sideboard with a brass rail gallery in the style of Sheraton, c.1780

Fig. 184 Mahogany chair with multi-splats decorated with rosettes and closed fans, c.1790

Fig. 185 Mahogany chair with sabre legs and panelled headrail, c.1810

Fig. 186 Mahogany chairs with turned front legs and ebony inlays, c.1800

definite upward curve before entering the back, Fig. 184. He was probably partly responsible for the design of the chair with the wide veneered panel head rail which is commonly called Regency, Fig. 185, and on this style of chair he shows the front legs either turned, Fig. 186, square turned, or square with the spade foot. He also shows them with the sabre leg, Fig. 187, a design which probably originated from the Greek and Egyptian designs of Thomas Hope and described more fully on page 95. In his easy chairs Sheraton designed both tub-shaped chairs with the low back and fully upholstered, Fig. 162, and also a high back chair with wings.

Settees by Sheraton are similar in style to those of Adam and Hepplewhite, Fig. 188, but he also has sofas which show definite signs of the influence of Hope's designs. Dining tables, oval and round in shape with turned, square-tapered, moulded or cabriole legs, were made during the Sheraton period. Around 1750, a gate-leg table was designed which was square or rectangular when open, with special clips on the edges of the leaves to which two D-shaped individual tables could be fixed to extend the length, Fig. 110 and 111, page 59-60. Towards the end of the eighteenth

Fig. 187 Sabre leg chair in grained rosewood and parcel-gilt, c.1810

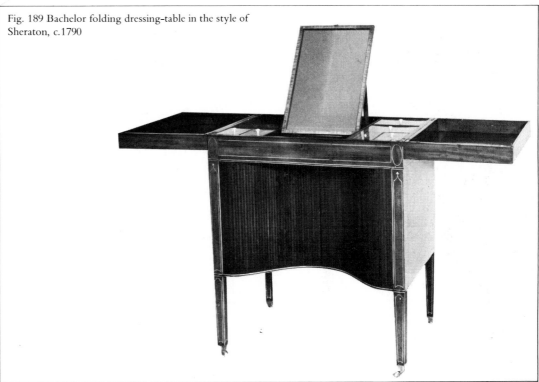

Fig. 189 Bachelor folding dressing-table in the style of Sheraton, c.1790

Fig. 188 Mahogany settee upholstered in leather in the style of Sheraton, c.1790

century tables were made up in separate sections with column splay-leg supports, usually with four legs not three, Fig. 112, page 60. Any number of these could be clipped together. The two end sections were usually half-round or D-shape.

Dressing, washing and writing tables by Sheraton have a great variety of shapes; round, square, kidney-shaped and also angled to fit a corner. A number of the dressing tables have

material draped round the front and sides and he used ingenious mechanical devices for fold-away mirrors, top extensions, reading stands and sun screens in his designs for these tables, Fig. 189 and 190. His designs for writing tables included the Carlton House table, Fig. 191 and his desks had fold-down cylinder or tambour tops which enclosed the writing surface, Fig. 192 and 193. Tripod tables are shown with one, two or three-tier tops and are also known as dumb waiters,

91

Fig. 190 Satinwood ladies worktable, c.1790

Fig. 191 'Carlton House' writing table made in mahogany, c.1800

Fig. 194. His designs for small occasional tables were many and varied; bedside tables with a cupboard for the chamber pot, tables with tilting tops for reading, tip-up-top tripod tables after the styles of Chippendale but with far less decoration, and Pembroke tables in the manner of Adam and Hepplewhite. Side tables and pier tables designed by Sheraton were similar to those of his contemporaries, Fig. 195.

Overmantle mirrors, rectangular in shape, are

shown with pilaster or column ends and with painted decoration on the glass friezes. Wall and toilet mirrors were in the same style as those of Hepplewhite, Fig. 179, page 85. He was probably partly responsible for popularising the circular convex plate mirror, circa 1800, which often has an eagle and acanthus cresting and ball or rosette decor round the mould, Fig. 196.

Bed designs by Sheraton have more material draping than those of Hepplewhite and are

similar, in fact, to those of the late walnut period but the posts and the carvings are much more delicate. He also designed twin-beds under the same canopy or tester.

Decoration
Thomas Sheraton, like the other designers of the period, favoured the classical style, using the acanthus leaf, urns, flower and material festoons on his friezes, rails, etc. He appears to have favoured delicate carving in preference to paint or inlay but he did use all three. The tops

Fig. 194 Mahogany dumb-waiter, c.1750

Fig. 193 Mahogany desk with tambour fall, c.1790

Fig. 195 Mahogany side table, c.1780

Fig. 192 Mahogany desk with cylinder fall, c.1800

of his chests and sideboards are often not moulded but square-edged and cross-banded. Hepplewhite also shows this on some of his furniture. The main moulds on cornices were decorated, usually just above the frieze, with dental, Greek key or ball and sausage bead, and the latter was also used below the frieze. Cornices by Chippendale and Hepplewhite show the same motifs. The square at the top of both turned and square legs on Sheraton sideboards and cabinets run right through to the top of the carcase in pilaster form. Some of the turned legs were in column form. The decoration on his chairs was mainly achieved with curl or similar veneers and cross-banded or with carving and moulding. He did use inlays but usually confined to banding or stringing. He used the same carved or moulded decoration on the legs of his chairs as Hepplewhite, but his legs were not quite as delicate. His low cabinets and chests of drawers were supported on either square, turned or plinth feet, mainly using the splay-toe plinth feet, Appendix 1, page 120.

Fig. 196 Gilded convex mirror with ball decoration and eagle cresting, c.1800

Fig. 197 Armchair polished and parcel-gilt, in the style of Thomas Hope, c. 1810

Fig. 198 Chair with cane seat and panel, the leg and back shape in the style of Thomas Hope, c.1810

Fig. 199 Chair with ebony and brass inlay and brass cup castors in the style of Hope, c.1810

The designs of Thomas Hope (1769–1831)

The designs of Hope are often called the Empire style and they have a rather clumsy appearance compared with the styles of other designers of the eighteenth century. They are ornately decorated and shaped showing Greek and Egyptian influence. His chairs often had sabre-shaped front legs and arm uprights and, when the back legs were also this shape, they were extended through to the head rail, Fig. 197, 198, 199 and 200.

Cabinets, though simple in construction, were clumsy in appearance with applied metal handles, mounts and decoration. The carcases of some of them, instead of being square, tapered in width from the bottom to the top. The designs by Hope are probably partly responsible for the return of more robust styles in furniture, which followed the elegant and delicate styles of the later part of the eighteenth century.

Thomas Hope favoured Greek and Egyptian styles and his designs can be recognised by this type of decoration. Legs were often carved in classical human or animal shapes, or cabriole with animal or human masks on the knees. The masks were also used on the arms of chairs and panels on the backs of settees, chairs, etc. were decorated with classical

Fig. 200 Chair with ormolu mounts and honeysuckle decoration in the back, c.1810

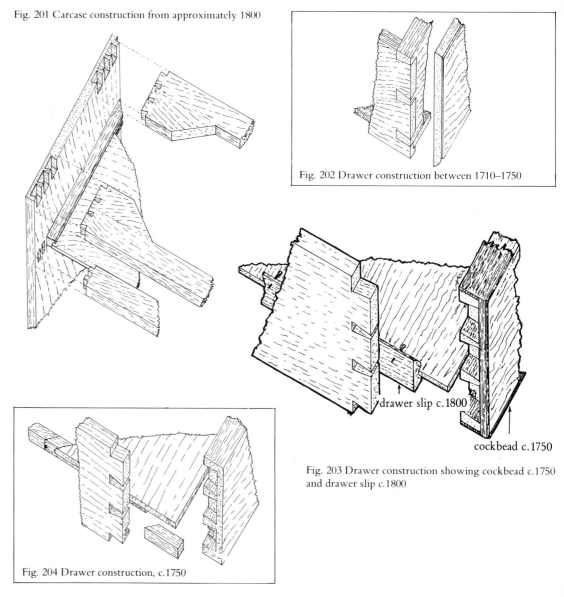

Fig. 201 Carcase construction from approximately 1800

Fig. 202 Drawer construction between 1710–1750

drawer slip c.1800

cockbead c.1750

Fig. 203 Drawer construction showing cockbead c.1750 and drawer slip c.1800

Fig. 204 Drawer construction, c.1750

figures. Parcel-gilt, together with polished, painted or ebonised finishes appear to have been the favoured ornamentation for his designs. He also used bronze castings known as ormolu, Fig. 200, for busts, masks and figures for corbels, feet, handles, etc. He was probably partly responsible for the return of brass inlaying which was popular in the Regency period, Fig. 199, and continued into the early Victorian.

Timbers

The timbers which were mainly used for decorative, veneered and other show-wood work were Cuban mahogany, satinwood, rosewood, sycamore, amboyna and thuya. American walnut was used for chairs, tables, and cabinet furniture from approximately 1725. Boxwood and the fruit woods were used for inlaying and marquetry and pear and sycamore were dyed various colours, red, green and black, for inlays. Other decorative timbers used occasionally in this period were sabicu, partridge, kingwood, calamander, coromandel, padouk, tulip and maple.

Timbers used for construction work were Honduras mahogany, birch, alder, ash, cedar, chestnut, elm, lime, maple and beech. The early Georgian case furniture was mainly constructed of deal with a small number of the better quality pieces of oak, all of which were veneered with mahogany or walnut. A few early cabinets and chests were made of solid Cuban mahogany. Around the middle of the eighteenth century, when it was more plentiful, Honduras mahogany was used for carcase work, and Cuban mahogany was used for veneers.

Solid timber was used in case construction throughout this period. Only in doors and other unsupported areas was frame and panel construction used. Carcase bottoms and top rails were now cloak dovetailed into the ends and double stump tenons gradually replaced the drawer rail method of dovetailing or housing in from the front of the carcase. Backs were made up of thin jointed boards instead of frames. Drawer runners were still ploughed into the sides at rail level and dust-boards were ploughed into the back of the drawer rails and into the runners. Early drawers had a small ovolo mould round their fronts and were rebated on the ends, top and bottom of the fronts so that the mould overlapped on to the carcase. The sides and front of the drawers were ploughed to receive the bottom, the sides were cloak dovetailed into the front and open dovetails were used at the back, Fig. 201. An alternative method was for the section of the drawer front which is moulded and standing proud, to be made of mahogany and a deal or oak backing piece fixed to it, to make up the thickness and to receive the dovetail, Fig. 202. The cockbead was also a popular decoration on drawers from the first quarter of the eighteenth century, Fig. 203. This was a lath with a half-round edge which was rebated into the edges of the drawer front, the half-round standing proud of the front. From about 1800 drawer slips were used; instead of the drawer sides being ploughed for the bottom, Fig. 204, a separate lath with a plough and a quarter-round top edge was used, Fig. 203.

Decoration

Fittings   Hinges in this period were mainly of the butt type which were fixed with screws and pins to the edge or back of the door so that only the butt showed. The early handles up to approximately 1750 had flat fret-edged plates with loop or swan-neck grips fixed by round bolts which were bored in the head to

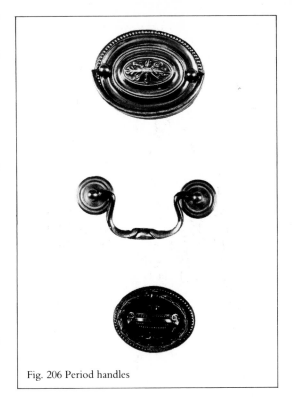

Fig. 206 Period handles

receive the pins of the grip, Fig. 96, page 51. The back plate was often pierced and sometimes engraved, Fig. 97, page 51. A handle dating from approximately the middle of the century had the swan-neck grip and separate ring back plate at each bolt, Fig. 206. In the later part of the Georgian period these handles had pressed or cast plates and grips with classical decoration. Around the last quarter of the eighteenth century, the plain plates and grips were superseded by cast brass

Fig. 205 Period handles

Fig. 207 Period knobs, handles and escutcheons

rococo-style plates and grips, Fig. 205. From around 1800, turned wood and stamped or cast brass knobs were used, Fig. 207. The knob grips were slim with bead or rosette decoration on the face and the wooden ones were sometimes inset with mother of pearl or ivory.

The early escutcheons were made to match the handle plates and were in the rococo style. In the later part of the Georgian period they either matched the plates of the handles or

were set in flush to the surface of the wood sometimes with just the beading standing proud. Ring grip handles, both round and oval in shape, with matching back plates, cast lion masks or similar, were used in the later part of the Georgian period.

Sheraton added brass rod galleries on his sideboards, straight or serpentine and scroll-shaped, with capitals surmounted by candle branches, or urn or

pomegranate-shaped finials. Acanthus leaf shapes made from brass sheet were also used to decorate the scrolls and serpentine-shaped rods.

Rotating castors were used on furniture in England from about 1700. These had hardwood wheels, usually made from boxwood, then about mid-century leather was used, but by the last quarter of the eighteenth century brass was mainly used for wheel

Fig. 208 Castors

Towards the end of the century, about 1780, stamped brass mounts and handle plates came into use and for a short period around 1800, brass open-fretted grills were used as door panels.

Polishing and finishing   Alkanet root dye and tripoli powder were still used in the Georgian period as they were in the walnut period. Red lead and other pigments were used in glue size for colouring backs and pine interiors in the later part of the period.

Egg-shell varnish, copal varnish mixed with wax, was applied to the surfaces with a brush and was then burnished with tripoli powder in a wax and turpentine paste until the necessary shine was achieved. This and other similar methods were used until around 1820 when the method of French polishing, applying shellac with a cloth and wadding rubber, was introduced into England. It is certain that shellac was used in England during the whole of the eighteenth century but it would have been applied with a brush, not by the French method.

English style lacquer, see walnut period page 52, was used for finishing furniture throughout the whole of the period and gilding, although a popular finish, was used with much more reserve in the later part of the century.

making. At about the same time castors were fitted on ormolu style brass mounts, paw or scroll feet designs, Fig. 208.

Although Chippendale and others used ormolu-style mounts on their early eighteenth century furniture it was not until around 1760 that they were made in any quantity in England. They were in the neo-classical style, leaf and floral or husk festoons, ram and lion masks or heads, urns, etc.

The Victorian period 1837-1901

Fig. 209 Low cupboard or sideboard, c.1850

There appears to have been very little change during William IV reign from the designs of the Georgian period, except perhaps for a reversion to rococo, Gothic and late Tudor influences which dominated the early Victorian furniture styles, along with versions of the neo-classic.

After the designs of the Georgian period, Victorian furniture is heavy and almost clumsy in appearance, with extreme ogee-shaped or crudely-turned cup and cover shaped legs. The spiral twist was also used and this, too, was crude compared with that on earlier furniture. The cabinet making generally shows a high degree of skill but lacks the elegance of the Georgian period styles. Although in the earlier periods, architects and designers were responsible for furnishing complete rooms on an individual basis, it becomes noticeable that in the Victorian period suites of furniture were made on a batch production basis for certain rooms. This applied particularly to the drawing room when sofas, low-seated easy chairs and sets of single chairs were all made to match; and the bedrooms, when wardrobes, dressing-tables, wash stands, pedestal cupboards and beds were made as a complete suite.

Cupboards, chests, cabinets and wardrobes

Cupboards, chiffoniers and cabinets had some similarity in shape to the commodes of the mid-eighteenth century, but instead of the flowing serpentine or bow lines of that period, the shape was broken by extra hollows and rounds. The low cupboards and cabinets were fitted with a high serpentine-shaped board on the back edge of the top which was ornamented with moulds and carving and often had a mirror fitted in it, Fig. 209.

Wardrobes were massive and constructed in three or four carcase sections, the plinth base and the cornice connecting the sections together. The main mould of the cornice was usually ogee-shaped mounted over a wide flat frieze with a narrow oval or ogee-shaped mould planted under the frieze. The side carcases were fitted out in a variety of ways. Some had just a hat shelf and hooks and rail which gave full length hanging space, and some had half length hanging space with pull-out trays or shelves occupying the rest of the compartment, both were enclosed by a door. The hinged edges of the wardrobe doors often had a laminated ovolo mould 75–100mm (3–4in) wide planted on them which brought the door frame forward. If it was a centre door, both edges were treated in this manner and the cornice and plinth were shaped to

match. The centre compartment could be fitted in any of these ways but, instead of the door having a wood panel it was usually fitted with a mirror. Alternatively, instead of a cupboard the centre could be a chest of drawers with a half-depth cupboard with mirror panel doors fixed on top of it, Fig. 210.

The sideboards, like the wardrobes, were large and often had a quarter-round ovolo-shaped moulding on the doors or carcase. They were fitted with a background like the low cabinets but this was usually much more elaborate and often included small shallow cupboards as well as mirror plates. Carving and ormolu were

Fig. 210 Victorian wardrobe

101

Fig. 211 Carved oak Victorian sideboard, c.1850

Fig. 212 Cabinet in a style popular at the time of the Great Exhibition, c.1851

Fig. 213 Chair with panelled headrail, c.1840

Fig. 214 Balloon-back chair with turned legs, c.1850

Fig. 215 Balloon-back chair with cabriole scroll legs, c.1860

used extensively for decoration of the sideboards, Fig. 211 and 212.

Chests of drawers were often made five or six drawers in height. The tops were usually thick in appearance and had square or flat-round cross-band edges, Fig. 230, page 109. The drawer below the top also acted as a frieze and was often ogee-moulded on its front. This frieze or drawer, which stood proud of the rest of the carcase, was supported each end by

carved corbels or by turned columns which were mounted on the plinth, or base. The chests were either mounted on turned bun or similar shaped feet, or on a plain, unmoulded plinth.

Chairs

Dining chairs in the early part of the Victorian period were generally heavy in appearance with more than ample seat area. The front legs were usually round-turned, square-turned or

octagon-turned and of taper and toe, or cup and cover shape. The chair backs were similar in style to those designed by Thomas Hope, Fig. 197 and 198, page 95, with a wide concave head rail which over-lapped the back legs, and a single horizontal splat of various widths and shapes, Fig. 213. Alternatively the backs had a moulded face head rail of serpentine and concave shape which fitted on the top of the matching moulded back legs. The single splat was often shaped, moulded and fitted so that it

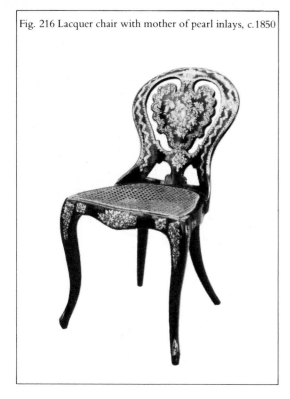

Fig. 216 Lacquer chair with mother of pearl inlays, c.1850

Fig. 217 Low easy or nursing chair, c.1850

Fig. 218 Chair in the style of Mackintosh, c.1900

completed a semi-oval shape back, Fig. 214 and 215. Around 1850, about the time of the Great Exhibition, chairs and other furniture became much more decorative, almost vulgar, with carved and ormolu ornament, gold leaf and inlay decoration using light woods, ivory and mother of pearl; also black and other colour lacquers on papier mâché, Fig. 216.

The designs for the easy chairs varied

considerably in style from the carved-cane or upholstered panel back, spiral twist or bobbin turned chairs of the walnut period, to those of the Adam or Kent period, with a certain amount of Gothic, rococo, Egyptian and Greek influence, and were much more solid in appearance. Bedroom and nursing chairs were similarly made but lower in the seat and usually without arms, Fig. 217, they were often made with spoon-shaped backs. It was not until around 1860 that lighter and more

delicate designs for chairs were seen and this was due to the influence of makers or designers such as Morris, Mackintosh, the Barnsleys, Gimson and Gillows, Fig. 218 and 219. Footstools were popular in the Victorian period. The early ones were usually composed of an ogee-moulded frame on bun feet but later they had rails and short, turned legs.

Fig. 219 Chair by Peter Waals in the style of Gimson and the Barnsleys

Fig. 221 Dining table with block base and round top, c.1840

Tables

Dining tables usually had round, oval or octagonal tops with a 75–100mm (3–4in) frieze rail planted under the outside edge, Fig. 220 and 221. They were supported by single or multi-turned columns on block and cabriole style legs, Fig. 222, or with a pillar-style veneered column on a base block with paw or bun feet. Alternatively a scotia or ogee-shaped veneered square column was used with paw feet. Some had tops which were hinged to pivot into a vertical position when not in use. Rectangular dining tables were in the style of the earlier sofa tables but without the folding leaves.

Side tables were made with either rectangular or serpentine-shaped tops which were usually supported by turned or cabriole legs at the front and either pilaster-type legs at the back or a panelled frame. They often had a row of drawers under the top or a rail, and these

Fig. 220 Table with block base, ormolu paw feet and brass inlays, c.1815

Fig. 222 Table with multi-column stand, c.1850

drawer fronts or rails were often moulded ogee or scotia-shaped. They usually had a backboard like the cupboards and often a shelf was fixed between the legs.

The card or gaming tables had a rail frame under the top and the top swivelled on this frame so that the flap top could be supported by it when it was open, Fig. 224. Tripod tea tables were mainly plain in design with an unmoulded tip-up top about 90cm (3ft) across

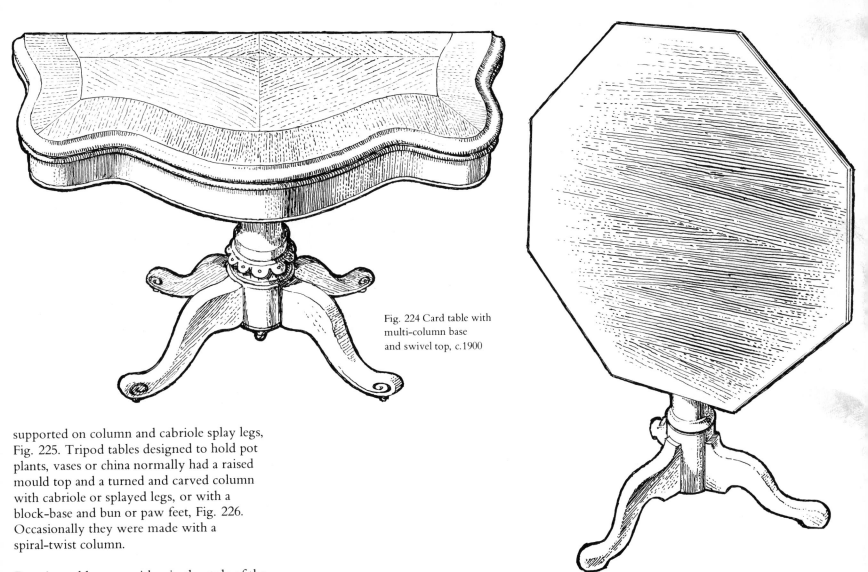

Fig. 224 Card table with
multi-column base
and swivel top, c.1900

supported on column and cabriole splay legs,
Fig. 225. Tripod tables designed to hold pot
plants, vases or china normally had a raised
mould top and a turned and carved column
with cabriole or splayed legs, or with a
block-base and bun or paw feet, Fig. 226.
Occasionally they were made with a
spiral-twist column.

Dressing-tables were either in the style of the
side tables or chest of drawers with a

Fig. 225 Tripod tea table with tip-up top, c.1800

Fig. 226 Vase or
plant pot stand, c.1840

Fig. 227 Whatnot with drawer, c.1800

Fig. 228 Whatnot to fit in a corner, c.1800

free-standing mirror, similar to the Georgian toilet mirrors, but much more solid in appearance. Wash tables were made to match the dressing-tables but had a marble top. Whatnots, a nest of shelves each supported by turned columns at the corners, were very popular at this period but date back to the beginning of the nineteenth century, Fig. 227 and 228. Ladies worktables in the Victorian period were supported by stands similar to the dining tables, Fig. 229.

Fig. 229 Victorian ladies worktable, c.1820

Wall mirrors were similar in style to those of the early eighteenth century with elaborate rococo decoration usually formed with compo not carved wood. Compo is a mix of whitening, resin and hot glue size poured or pressed into a previously prepared wood or plaster of Paris mould. The mould was black-leaded to prevent the compo from sticking to it. Toilet mirrors were usually mounted with the standards on a serpentine-shaped block with bun feet or with a box base with one or more lift-up lids. The mirror frame mould was flat-round or ogee-shaped. Convex wall mirrors were still being made and the decoration, again, was usually compo.

Beds
Beds in the early Victorian period were similar to those of the walnut period but were usually constructed in mahogany rather than oak or walnut. Around the period of the Great Exhibition beds began to be made in metal, iron and brass, and towards the end of the period these beds were made without the tall posts and canopy and only had high head and foot ends which had floral and scroll-shaped cast metal decoration.

Timber
Timbers used for construction were ash, beech, birch, cedar, elm, Honduras and Cuban mahogany, maple, oak, plane, rosewood, satinwood, sycamore and deal. Timbers used for inlaying and decorative veneered work were mahogany, walnut, chestnut, kingwood, maple, rosewood, satinwood, boxwood, tulipwood, yew, ebony and the fruit woods.

Construction
In the early Victorian period machines came into general use, and although mass production came later, a certain amount of batch production took place as a result.

Frame construction on carcase work was used again, but instead of the panels being ploughed

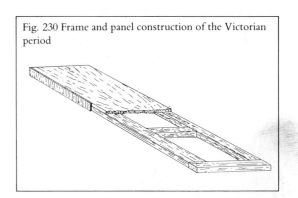

Fig. 230 Frame and panel construction of the Victorian period

into the frame, they were usually planted on, covering the frame. This method was frequently used for tops, and the edges were then veneered or had a mould planted round them, Fig. 230. Backs were usually frames with ploughed in panels and drawers were hand-dovetailed with the grain of the bottoms running from side to side and usually fixed with drawer-slips, see Georgian construction, Fig. 203, page 96. If the drawers were very wide the drawer bottoms were made in two pieces with a ploughed muntin support in the centre running from the front to the back of the drawer. Plinth bases for cabinets were usually made as a separate frame and fixed with screws and glue blocks. Dust-boards, instead of being level with the tops of the drawer rails and runners, were now usually about 6–20mm (¼–⅜in) thick, fitting into a plough in the centre of the edge of the rails and runners.

In chair construction both mortice and tenon and dowel joints were used. In dining chair seat construction the method most often used was similar to that used in the Regency period see page 00. The side rails were made level with the upholstery and the seat frame finished flush with the front edge of the front rail and was held in position with a wood or metal pin, Fig. 187, page 91.

Decoration

The top quality furniture of the early part of this period, particularly around the time of the Great Exhibition, was profusely ornamented with floral, festoon, figure and pillar decoration carved in wood, stamped from sheet brass or copper or cast in brass or plaster, Fig. 212, page 102. Surfaces were inlaid using various coloured woods, marble, mother of pearl, Fig. 231, and ivory. China plaques decorated with classical figures were also used, but these were about the limit of painted decoration until the 1860's.

The wood carving of this time, although mainly in high relief, did not have the freedom and life-like style of that of the eighteenth century. There was too much uniformity in the designs and frequently insufficient care was given to detail.

Metal castings, however, had improved considerably on those of the mid-eighteenth century and the fettling or finish was much cleaner. They too, like the wood carving, had a certain amount of uniformity in design which gave an unnatural appearance to leaf and floral decoration.

Fig. 231 Side table with panel end supports, c.1870

Fretwork was used on chairs and tables and also for cabinet panels, and it was either plain-faced or ornamented with carving. On chairs, in particular, this had rather a flat appearance when compared with the carving on the earlier walnut chairs.

The more ordinary furniture of this period was sparsely decorated with carving and depended mainly on figured veneers to enhance its appearance. Tops on chests, sideboards and cabinets were usually thick with a square or flat-round cross-band veneered edge and the top edges of plinths were mostly left square, not moulded. Columns at the outside front edges were plain turnings and some cabinets and chests had fluted flat pilasters or carved corbels under the ogee or scotia-shaped frieze which could sometimes be composed of a drawer or drawers, Fig. 209, page 100. The doors had either an ogee or ovolo-shaped mould planted round the sunken panels. These

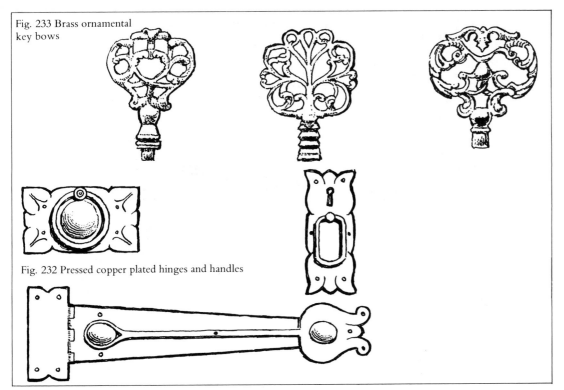

Fig. 233 Brass ornamental key bows

Fig. 232 Pressed copper plated hinges and handles

panels were sometimes dome-shaped at the top and were also decorated with small floral or leaf carvings. Backboards had moulding planted round outside, serpentine-shaped front edges and they, too, often had a little planted carving on the face. Pediments on wardrobes and similar furniture were similar in shape and decoration to the cabinet backboards.

Another type of decoration used in this period was poker or pen work whereby designs were burnt into the timber with a hot needle. This was probably the work of ladies of leisure and not done by craftsmen.

Fittings Butt hinges were mainly used but on the decorated lacquer furniture the ornamental brass face-fixing type of hinge was often used. In the latter part of the period stamped metal, copper-plated handles and face-fixing hinges came into general use, Fig. 232.

Machine-turned, parallel-shank screws with no point were used until a short time before 1850

when Nettlefold brought out a machine for making pointed screws with tapered shanks. Up to this date screws were usually made of brass for interior work and hinge fixing, but from the mid-nineteenth century iron screws were mainly used, except when fixing handles and face-fixing hinges when brass or copper finished metal screws were used.

Turned wood knobs were used throughout the whole of the Victorian period, but unlike the slim-face decorated knobs of the Regency period, they were thicker on the grip and usually only domed on the face. The earlier knobs were fixed with a metal pin with a nut threaded on to the rear end. Later they were fixed with a wood pin, approximately 12mm (½in) thick, which was screwed and tapped into the knob, and which had a head that fitted up to the back of the drawer or door.

A number of the more elaborate cabinets of this period, as well as some of the more utility ones, have locks fixed with ornamental-headed keys, Fig. 233 and escutcheons, or to have concealed hand grips in the woodwork instead of having handles to open the drawers and doors. In the second half of the nineteenth century handles mainly reverted back to the loop or ring type but with the grip swivel-socket riveted to the back plate and the backplate face-fixed with screws. On cupboard doors handlegrips were fitted to a square spindle which operated the latch section of the lock. The back plates of the better quality handles were still cast in brass, Fig. 234, the cheaper handles had stamped steel plates, copper

Fig. 234 Handles and castors

plated. This type of copper finish was also used for the ornamental face-fixing hinges which were fitted in the later part of the period.

Coil springs had been used in upholstery from around 1800 but now came into general use.

As well as the brass wheel castors, Fig. 208, composition stone wheel castors were introduced in the Victorian period, Fig. 234.

Polishing and Finishing Gilding was not as popular for furniture decoration as it had been earlier and in the latter part of the period it seems to have been mainly confined to mirror and picture frames.

Water stains were in general use in this period and these included vandyke crystals, to which a little ammonia was usually added, umber, lamp black or red lead, which were mixed with a thin glue-size, and the fumes composing ·880 ammonia, potassium bichromate and sodium carbonate. Aniline dyes were used, sometimes mixed with water but more often mixed with methylated spirits, and then only used for matching up and colouring small areas.

Wax polishing was now very seldom used, instead shellac was in general use, mainly applied by the French method described on page 99. Lacquer was still used, particularly on papier mâché work, but painted decoration was only used occasionally.

Graining, a technique using coloured pigment mixed with turpentine and oil and applied to imitate the figure of timber, was used from the beginning of the nineteenth century instead of veneering, when mahogany, rosewood, and walnut were simulated, particularly on cabinet-ends, but also on chairs and other furniture, obviously to reduce the cost.

Grain filling, before polishing, was achieved by making up a paste consisting of whitening, colour pigments such as umber, red lead or lampblack, raw linseed oil, turpentine and tallow. Sometimes plaster of Paris was used instead of whitening, but it was difficult to use because it dried out so quickly. The grain filler was applied with a circular action, usually using a pad of hessian or sacking rather than a brush. After leaving it for a short period the surplus filler was removed from the surface of the timber with a clean piece of hessian. For some reason, over a period of time, the colour pigments tended to suck back leaving only the whitening showing and this white in the grain is most noticeable in mahogany.

The Edwardian period 1901–1910

Fig. 235 Edwardian sideboard, c.1900

Furniture in the later part of the Victorian period developed along more delicate lines and the designers of the Edwardian period continued this by reverting back to more elegant styles similar to those of the late Georgian period. As in the Victorian period, complete suites of furniture were made for furnishing bedrooms, drawing rooms and dining rooms.

Dining room suites were usually made in either oak or mahogany. Sideboards were similar in design to the dressers of the seventeenth century, with a row of drawers at the top and cupboards in the lower section, Fig. 235. The central cupboard door was often set back forming a knee-hole recess. The cabinets had ornate backboards with mirror panels and a moulded cornice which was supported at the front with either brackets or turned columns Fig. 236. These columns often supported shelves or small cupboards.

113

Fig. 237 Edwardian single chair, c.1910

Fig. 236 Edwardian cabinet, c.1900

Dining chair backs were either head height – with a splat or multi-splats or shoulder height with a head rail which was usually carved or an upholstered back panel, Fig. 237. The front legs of the dining chairs were either square or turned, with a spade foot.

The dining tables were usually square or rectangular in shape with turned and fluted or reeded legs with a spade foot. Many of them were made to extend by fitting an edge up

Fig. 239 Edwardian easy chair, *en suite* with Fig. 237 and 238

Fig. 238 Edwardian settee, *en suite* with Fig. 237

frame inside the main rails which was fixed to one end of the table. The main rails were fixed to the other end. The top was in two halves with one half fixed to each of these sections.

The sections were connected together with a tongue and groove slide in the centre and between the inner rails and outer main rails. They were usually extended by turning a long metal screw, fitting under the table from end to end, with a separate handle, which forced

the two sections of the table away from each other, thus allowing extra leaves to be fitted into the top.

The drawing room suites, though sometimes made of oak, walnut or mahogany, were more usually made of beech which was stained to resemble dark oak, walnut or mahogany. They were composed of a sofa or settee, Fig. 238, and two easy chairs and often a number of single chairs, Fig. 237. The sofa had a scroll

upholstered head end and a low padded back rail fixed to the head and running the overall length which was supported by a number of turned spindles and a lower rail which in turn was fixed at the foot end to a bracket-shaped support connecting the back seat rail and the padded rail. The easy chairs were made in show-wood style with the back legs extending beyond the head rail and usually finishing in a scroll, Fig. 239. The head rail had either an upholstered pad or was carved and fitted above a pin-cushion upholstered back frame. The arms were padded and constructed in the same manner as the sofa backs or settee. The front legs were usually turned and the seats had show-wood rails and built-up, coil-sprung upholstery.

Single chairs, usually six or eight in number, were made to dining chair seat height with backs similar to the easy chairs, but without arms, Fig. 237. All seat furniture was usually fitted with castors.

Small ladies boudoir or drawing room suites were made in mahogany or walnut and usually comprised two easy chairs and a settee. Though smaller, they were similar in style to the suite described above, with pin-cushion upholstery and spindle backs, pad and spindle arms. Instead of moulding and carving on their show-wood areas, they were inlaid with floral decoration and line inlays. The legs were usually square-tapered with a spade toe and these were also inlaid. The settees were in the same style as the chairs but were extended in width to seat two or three people.

Bedroom suites were made of oak, mahogany, ash, veneeered walnut or satin walnut, called red gum in South America where it was grown. The three-door wardrobes were much less cumbersome than those of the earlier Victorian period, and the ends as well as the doors often were of frame and panel construction. Often the panels in the frames were fielded and the centre door was sometimes fitted with a mirror panel instead of

wood. The interiors of the larger wardrobes were usually fitted out in a similar manner to those of the Victorian period.

The two-door wardrobes often had a fixed panel between the doors, fitted with a mirror plate. Some were made of two-tier carcase construction, the lower carcase fitted with one or more drawers. Wardrobes were also made with a single door, usually with a mirror panel. The width of the front was made up with solid pilasters on each side of the door, or with panelled frames and the bottom carcase was usually fitted with one large, deep drawer.

Dressing-tables were usually nests of drawers, often with a knee-hole in the centre. Triple mirrors were usually fixed on the backboard which also supported small jewel drawers and shelves. If the wardrobe of the suite was not fitted with a mirror, the centre of the dressing-table was only the plinth or one drawer high in the centre and had a full length swivel mirror fitted.

Wash stands were similar in construction to the knee-hole dressing-tables, and often had chamber pot cupboards instead of, or as well as, drawers.

Beds were made with framed ends and flat or fielded panels, or vertical splats whichever was suitable to match the rest of the suite.

Occasional Furniture
Drawing room and library tables were usually oval or round in shape, the round ones often

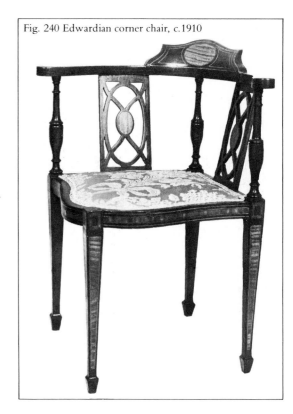

Fig. 240 Edwardian corner chair, c.1910

being similar to the earlier drum tables but smaller. The oval style tables were smaller and similar to Victorian dining tables, page 105. The tops were inlaid with lines and floral decoration and the rails fitting round the under edge of the top were inlaid and usually had serpentine-shaped bottom edges. These tables were usually veneered with walnut.

Individual arm chairs were made at dining chair seat height with inlaid showwood

Fig. 241 Edwardian piano stool, c.1910

Fig. 242 Edwardian ladies worktable, c.1900

Fig. 243 Edwardian occasional table, c.1900

splatted backs. Chairs designed to fit in a corner were also made in this style, Fig. 240. These chairs were probably used in the drawing room or library for writing, or in the hall.

Stools generally appear to have been out of fashion at this period, apart from foot stools and those for the piano, Fig. 241.

Worktables were usually square or octagonal

in shape with a tapering box compartment and hinged, lift-up lid, Fig. 242, and often stood on carved ogee-shaped canted legs. They were mainly walnut-veneered and inlaid, and some of the tops were inlaid to use as games boards.

Small, rectangular, square, round and oval tables were made, usually with stretcher rails supporting a small shelf, Fig. 243. They had boxwood inlay and line decoration. Tripod stands for plants, flowers or china appear to

have gone out of favour at this period and they were replaced with stands with square or round tops supported by four slim, square, tapered legs connected by narrow rails under the top, and with cross-stretchers or a shelf in the lower half. They, too, were decorated with inlays.

Small writing tables made in this period had flat tops with a velvet or leather writing area and with a nest of drawers along the back

117

Fig. 244 Edwardian china cabinet, c.1910

edge, rather like those of the eighteenth century.

Desks were made in table form with a row of drawers underneath, and the flat writing area had a nest of drawers at the back enclosed by a drop-down cylinder front or tambour. Writing cabinets were in the form of shelves with a drop-flap writing area, and sometimes the upper shelves, above the writing flap was enclosed by doors.

China cabinets were of frame construction with glass panels at the front and sides, made with straight, bow or serpentine-shaped fronts and were supported on tapered legs, with or without the spade foot. They were decorated with floral and line inlays, Fig. 244.

Timber
Timbers used for construction in this period were oak, mainly American but some European and Japanese; walnut, again mainly American but some European; satin-walnut; American and African mahogany; ash; chestnut and deal. Timbers used for decorative purposes such as veneering and inlaying were mahogany, walnut, sycamore, rosewood, satinwood, maple, boxwood and the fruit woods.

Construction
Carcase work at this period reverted back almost completely to frame and panel construction. The solid carcase tops and bottoms on wardrobes were usually rebated and screwed into the end frames. Most of the

bottoms of other carcases were also fixed this way or were ploughed into the sides and fixed with glued blocks. The ogee-moulded and flat-frieze cornices on wardrobes and cabinets were planted loose on the tops and held in position with corner blocks glued to the carcase. The bases, too, were separate on the larger pieces of furniture and fixed in the same way.

On small wardrobes instead of the door being fitted with butt hinges it was often hung with pivot-pin hinges which connected into the cornice and the base carcase.

Dowel joints were used frequently throughout the whole of this period, particularly for chair making. The dowels were turned out in convenient lengths by machine and were usually made from beech or alder.

Decoration

Although moulding was mainly confined to tops and cornices in the Edwardian period, multiple beads were often worked through the centre of the drawer fronts, on door and frame stiles and on the upper square of the legs. At times a small ogee mould was worked round the edges of the drawer fronts, but planted moulds and cockbeads are seldom seen.

Fielded panels were a common form of decoration and these were normally fitted into square-edges frames, not moulded as they were in earlier periods.

Carving was used with a certain amount of reserve and was confined to decorating chair headrails, incised or shallow relief carving on small panels in doors and other frames, and sometimes to cornices, particularly those on the sideboard overmantles and also to corbels and brackets.

Turning in spindle form at the head of the upholstered seat backs and under the arm pads of chairs, as well as for occasional tables, sideboards and dressing tables.

Veneering is mainly seen on the more expensive bedroom suites, when burr walnut or mahogany curls were used. Oak sideboards were often veneered with pollard or brown oak, mahogany sideboards with curls or fiddleback veneers, and figured or burr veneers were used on walnut sideboards. The less expensive sideboards, which were probably batch produced, were seldom veneered and usually made of solid satin-walnut, mahogany or oak.

The less expensive bedroom suites were not usually veneered and were probably also made on a batch production basis. Satin-walnut, oak, mahogany or ash were the timber mainly used and the decoration on most of the suites was confined to small carved panels and reeding.

The better quality furniture in mahogany or walnut was inlaid with boxwood or sycamore lines, and panels of floral inlay. This particularly applied to the boudoir suites, china and other cabinets, occasional tables and chairs as well as some bedroom suites.

Fittings   Both the pressed and cast variety of butt hinge was in general use in this period, but the pivot hinge was used for wardrobe and large cupboard doors. The ornate face-fixing hinge was also still in use in the early part of the period. Most of the handle plates were stamped out of brass or steel which was then plated with a copper finish, Fig. 232, page 111. They were decorated with impressed neo-classical decoration, the grips being cast in either steel or brass and these were fixed by riveting the socket bolts to the back plate or, as in the Victorian period, on some of the cupboard handles the grip was fixed to a spindle which worked the latch in the lock. Most of the handles were face-fixed by screws through the plate. Handles were cast in brass for some of the better quality furniture and these also were normally face-fixed with screws.

Escutcheons were usually stamped out of steel or brass and face-fixed with screws although a small number were of cast brass. Brass knobs both stamped and cast were used but wood knobs do not appear to have been very popular. Locks were mainly made of brass and some had the escutcheon made in with the lock.

Polishing and finishing   The methods and materials used in this period were unchanged from those used in the Victorian period.

Appendix I

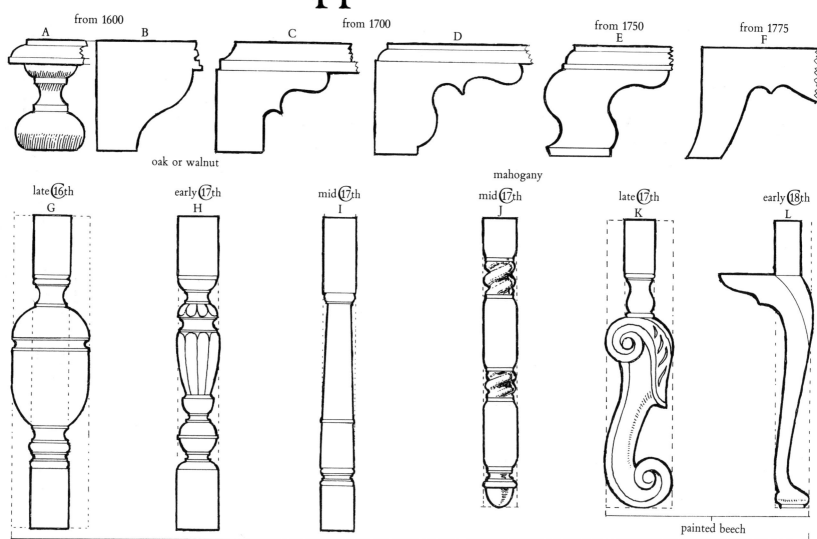

from 1600

A B

oak or walnut

from 1700

C D

mahogany

from 1750

E

from 1775

F

late (16)th
G

early (17)th
H

mid (17)th
I

mid (17)th
J

late (17)th
K

early (18)th
L

painted beech

oak and walnut

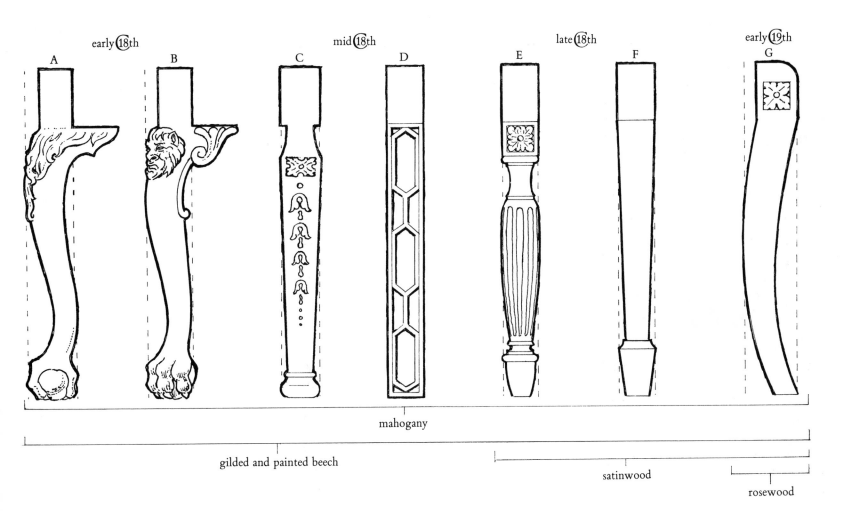

early **18**th   mid **18**th   late **18**th   early **19**th

A   B   C   D   E   F   G

mahogany

gilded and painted beech

satinwood

rosewood

Upholstery

Early sixteenth century upholstery work was mainly confined to beds and bedding, though a small number of cushions were made to use on the wood-seat chairs. The covers were often of linen or canvas embroidered with needlework, but velvet, damask, and satin was also used. Occasionally cow-hide was stretched across the seat area instead of wood.

Cushions and bedding were filled with either feathers, down, hay, or straw. Hair and wool were also sometimes used but the use of these was not considered to be very sanitary until about the middle of the century when special regulations came out which made sure they were more hygenic.

Bed mattresses were often supported by boring the side and end rails and threading rope criss-cross between them. Otherwise canvas or linen was stretched across and either fixed with rope looped through it and into the rails or with hand-made tacks.

Towards the end of the sixteenth century upholstery began to play a much more important role and beds, in particular, were covered and hung with elaborate floral needlework.

In the early part of the seventeenth century there was a rapid increase in the use of upholstery for decorative purposes as well as for comfort. Beds, in particular, were elaborately ornamented with needlework-covered headboards, head curtains, pelmets, bedspreads and draw curtains. In the last quarter of the century the whole of the tester or canopy was often covered with ornate needlework or patterned velvet which was further ornamented with fringes, tassel trimmings, gimp and braid. The tester was usually surmounted with material covered corner finials with ostrich feathers used as part of the trimming. The bed posts were also covered with material instead of being carved.

The chairs in the early part of the seventeenth century mainly had loose cushions laid on a stretched canvas or linen base fixed to the rails. Velvet, needlework or silk was used to cover the rails and backs and in some cases the whole of the woodwork was covered and, like the beds, trimmed with fringes, tassels, gimps and braids. Brass dome-headed nails were usually used to fix the trimming. Stools were treated in the same manner as the chairs but the cushion was usually fixed to the under canvas.

From approximately 1620 chairs were made with fixed upholstery on the seats and backs, the stuffing was spread evenly over the stretched linen or canvas base and a second piece of canvas or linen tacked over the top of it to keep it in place. The needlework, velvet or silk damask was then fixed, usually in such a way that it could easily be removed for repairs and cleaning.

Not until about the middle of the seventeenth century was a stitched roll used on top of the chair rails, this was made by allowing the stretched base canvas to overhang the rails by appoximately 75mm (3in), this was folded back over the rails and the fold filled with hay or straw, the loose edges were then stitched to the base canvas. Wool, hay, hair or straw was then spread evenly between the rolls and linen or canvas fixed over to hold it in place. Webbing appears to have come into use towards the end of the century, but it has not been possible to date it accurately.

Double stuffing came into use around 1730;

webbing and canvas was stretched over the seat rails and horse-hair was then spread evenly over and a canvas fixed with tacks on top. The canvas was then stitched from approximately the edge of the rails through to the top, the needle coming out about 50mm (2in) from where it entered. The needle is then entered again at right-angles to the first stitch and about 50mm (2in) away from it and coming out at the edge of the rail again, the twine is drawn through but leaving approximately a 100mm (4in) loop on the top side. A third stitch is then entered at the rail edge through to the top and the loop left at the second stitch is passed over needle, the twine is then drawn tight to form a cylindrical roll over the rails, a regulating needle being used to make sure that the roll is evenly filled with hair; the loops left at both top and rail edge giving a continuous stitch which holds the hair in the roll. A second layer of hair is then placed on top between the rolls, covered with a thin layer of wool, and a canvas fixed by tacking on to the rails before covers of either painted satin, silk, velvet, damask, needlework, brocade or leather.

Buttoned upholstery appears about 1780, but the deep buttoning popular in the Victorian period was only used after the coil spring came into use about 1800. At this time, also, multiple stitching of the edges of the upholstery to make them stand vertically above the frame was in fairly general use although this dates back to about 1760.

Acknowledgements

For permission to use the following photographs the Publishers gratefully acknowledge:

Bonsor Pennington Fig. 30, 235, 236

The Council for Small Industries in Rural Areas Fig. 2, 15, 16, 17, 23, 24, 26 (left), 44, 53, 54, 58, 59, 62, 63, 66, 67, 68, 69, 70, 71, 76, 79, 81, 82, 89, 90, 117, 118, 119, 120, 121, 122, 123, 133, 134, 136, 137, 138, 139, 140, 144, 154, 155, 156, 159, 160, 161, 163, 164, 187, 188, 193, 195, 198, 199, 200, 217, 220, 242.

Leicestershire Museum and Art Gallery Fig. 219

Mallet Fig. 10, 18, 19, 31, 33, 34, 46, 50, 55, 56, 64, 72, 75, 77, 84, 91, 99, 100, 101, 102, 105, 107, 108, 110, 111, 112, 113, 114, 115, 116, 124, 132, 142, 143, 149, 158, 165, 166, 171, 172, 173, 174, 175, 176, 177, 179, 184, 185, 191, 197.

H. E. Savill Fig. 96, 97, 205, 206, 207, 208

Sotheby's Belgravia Fig. 218, 237, 238, 239, 244

Stair & Co. Ltd. Fig. 7, 17, 21, 27, 28, 29

The Victoria & Albert Museum Fig. 4, 5, 6, 11, 20, 22, 25, 26 (right), 32, 35, 36, 47, 51, 52, 60, 61, 65, 73, 74, 78, 85, 95, 98, 103, 109, 125, 127, 128, 130, 131, 141, 145, 147, 162, 167, 190, 194, 196, 211, 212, 213, 214, 215, 216, 222, 227, 229, 231

Index

Padouk

Kingwood

Tulipwood

Plane

East Indian Rosewood

Brazilian Rosewood

Macassar Ebony

Coromandel